REPUBLIC EARTH ORGANISATION

Contents

INTRODUCTION

Ω

In the 21st century we are experiencing an exciting transition into a global society. This transition will open up enormous opportunities for all citizens around the world.

In Melbourne, Australia, people speak over 260 languages from over 200 countries, believing in over 135 different faiths. Melbourne is truly a multicultural city, and is fast becoming a Global Capital of the 21st century.[1] I believe Melbourne and Australia can play a leading role in helping to create a successful transition to a globalised society.

As a member of the Australian Labor Party in 2019, I wish to introduce a new political concept, called Republic Earth. I believe this concept can help make sense of the globally interconnected world we now live in.

Republic Earth aims to create a sense of order in the 21st century by celebrating democracy as humanity's finest achievement, and by creating a global democracy whereby everybody's voice is heard. As we create a globalised society, or a Republic Earth, we need to do all we can to bring people together for the common good, rather than see a more fractured world emerge.

Recently, there was a growing discussion about a political divide between globalisation and nationalism; however, this discussion is not quite right. To make sense of the 21st century, *New York Times* journalist Thomas Freidman has a really captivating idea. Freidman suggests that the 20th century was a battle between capitalism and communism, whereas the 21st century is a battle between order and disorder.[2]

On the one hand, we have a new **World of Order** emerging in the form of the creation of a global society, and on the other hand, at the same time, we have a new **World of Disorder** emerging in the form of an increase in global challenges that the world has to address. The goal now is for nations and citizens to work together to create a new World of Order, which means creating a successful globalised society or a Republic Earth that benefits all citizens around the world. But first let's learn more about this battle between order and disorder that is defining the 21st century.

CHAPTER 1: WORLD OF ORDER

We have witnessed, since this century began, an exciting new **World of Order** emerge. This **World of Order** is the continual journey to create a globalised society, which I like to call a Republic Earth. People can call this globalised society what they like, but the key point to understand is that the world is going global and we need to embrace the new **World of Order**. For example, over the last 19 years we have witnessed the following:

- Over half of the world's 7.7 billion people have access to the internet, and within 15 years the whole world will be interconnected. Mark Zuckerberg's Facebook is committed to building a global online community and it now has over two billion users.[3]

- More people have entered the world's middle class, especially in countries such as China and India, and thus developing countries are becoming developed. In 1980, China had the largest number of impoverished people on Earth. Since then it has lifted more than 800 million people above the poverty line; more than half its population.[4] We are also experiencing an increase in free trade; however, we need more fair-trade policies that aim to benefit more people.

- More people have access to better education, better health outcomes and better job opportunities on a global scale. Most people today live in cities. Just 600 cities, including 30 megacities, account for two-thirds of global GDP.[5] We live in an age of human capital and we need to maximise everyone's human potential.

- We are also witnessing a growing trend to end all forms of discrimination against women and girls everywhere and achieve the goal of gender equality. The global #MeToo campaign is seeing women calling out their own experiences of sexual harassment in the workplace and domestic violence at home. We are also witnessing the need to end racial discrimination through the Black Lives Matter campaign. We need to eliminate racial and gender inequality on a global scale.

- We are witnessing improvements in agricultural production and a move to a more localised and ecological-based agricultural system. We are also seeing a movement away from meat production towards a plant-based form of food production.

- The world is undergoing a transition to a renewable energy economy and the creation of a global sustainable society. More than 45 countries are committed to 100 per cent renewable energy.[6] In 2015, the G7 leaders decided to phase out fossil fuel emissions this century.[7] Widespread use of fusion energy in the 21st century could be a game changer for the renewable energy economy. We are also starting to see a great unravelling occurring from an industrial growth society to a life-sustaining society.

- We have now built a global, interconnected, joint-ventured economy. A car could easily just be assembled in the United States after its engine, tyres and other components have been made in countries around the world.

- Young people, through technology, are able to access better training to gain technical skills, and in the future young people who wish to obtain a qualification will have access to all subjects, all courses and all lecturers from any university in the world. We already see students in China and Japan involved online in Michael J. Sandal's Ethics Class at Harvard University in the US.[8]

- On a global scale we are seeing people living longer and having better health outcomes. We are also seeing many hospitals and research facilities working together to cure diseases. For example, 25 research facilities in 19 countries are working on the Human Proteome Project to identify all of the proteins in the human body, which could have massive ramifications in potentially curing cancers or major diseases.[9]

- People all around the world are enjoying a new world of entertainment where in the not-too-distant future they will have access to any music, TV show, film or live sporting event from anywhere in the world. As part of the Republic Earth Organisation, we are currently campaigning to create a global communications network that allows you to access any national television station live through the internet to your home, and to have all the world's entertainment made available to everyone around the world.

- We are also witnessing a new global renaissance emerge as over the coming years the 7.7 billion people in the world become fully interconnected. This will mean coming into contact with over 6,000 languages, 4,300 religions, 370 million indigenous people living in 90 countries around the world and everyone exchanging an explosion of new ideas globally, instantly and at zero cost.[10]

- There is a growing respect for indigenous rights, and we must continue to do more to respect the inherent rights and titles of our first peoples. Indigenous communities have been at the forefront of protecting rivers, coasts, forests and lands from out-of-control industrial activity. We can bolster this role, and reset our relationship globally, by fully implementing the United Nations Declaration on the Rights of Indigenous Peoples.

- To succeed with making this globalised society or Republic Earth a success, we need to bring people together for the common good. We need to embrace and celebrate the wonderful diversity of humanity.

Republic Earth Organisation

- As part of the Republic Earth Organisation, we are committed to starting this process of bringing the world together for the common good via a Republic Earth Music Festival, to be held on New Year's Eve each year. The aim is to allow citizens to vote for their favourite song of the year and then to have the popular songs performed on stage. We believe music unites people, so a Republic Earth Music Festival could unite the world.

- As this new **World of Order** emerges, we need to ensure that all citizens around the world can benefit from the new opportunities this globalised world offers.

CHAPTER 2: WORLD OF DISORDER

However, on the other hand, this century we have also witnessed a new **World of Disorder** emerge and a breakdown occur of the **World of Order**. For example, over the last 19 years we have witnessed the following:

- Growing threats of climate change, as we have placed over 30 per cent more CO_2 into the atmosphere than at any time in the last 800,000 years, and, as a result, we are witnessing an increase in climate change natural disasters.[11] In 2017, we saw record flooding in Namibia, record flooding in Houston, record flooding and drought in Peru, record low levels of global sea ice in the Arctic and Antarctic, and the hottest summer in cities like Brisbane and Sydney in Australia.[12] The biggest threat to our emerging global society is climate change, and it has the potential to be as destabilising as a global conflict.

- We are experiencing an increase in the rate of animal extinction. Since 1970, despite growing ecological awareness, wildlife populations have halved. In 1980, there were 2 billion wild birds in Europe. Scientists estimate that we're now losing species at 1,000 to 10,000 times the background rate, with literally dozens going extinct every day.[13] It could be a scary future indeed, with as many as 30 to 50 per cent of all species potentially heading toward extinction by mid-century.[14]

- We are experiencing an increase in environmental degradation in the form of deforestation, and we are experiencing a plastic pollution epidemic in our oceans.

- We are experiencing an increase in the number of displaced people and refugees, which now totals over 68 million people worldwide.[15]

- We are experiencing an increase in terrorism and terrorist attacks, as evidenced by recent attacks in Manchester,

London, Kabul, Baghdad and Melbourne. In 2017, over 11,000 terrorist attacks occurred in more than 100 countries.[16]

- We are experiencing an increase in global security threats, especially threats posed by nations such as North Korea through its missile testing.

- We are experiencing an increase in crime rates in cities around the world, and people feeling less safe in their own communities. A combination of unemployment, lack of education and being male in cities is, unfortunately, leading to 500,000 people dying each year via violent crimes such as homicide.[17] Our goal should be to radically reduce homicidal violence.

- We are experiencing an increase in health outbreaks in the form of the Ebola and Zika viruses.

- We are experiencing an increase in the breakdown of nations such as Syria and Yemen to the three forces of global warming, terrorism and refugees, all rapidly metastasising and feeding off of each other.

- We are experiencing an increase in deaths from obesity and diabetes (globally 1.5 million people died from diabetes in 2012) and sugar is now more dangerous than deaths by guns.[18]

- Partly due to the rise in technology, we are experiencing an increase in depression, suicide (globally 800,000 committed suicide in 2012) and other mental health disorders among young people in particular, as well as an increase in addictions such as to drugs, alcohol, pornography and gambling online.[19]

- People are living much longer than expected, and there is not enough money to pay for their pensions, medical treatment and aged care services.

- We are experiencing an increase in global inequality as the top one per cent own more than half the world's wealth.[20]

Introduction

- We are experiencing an increase in protectionist economic policies and a growing unease with free trade. We are experiencing an increase in nations like Russia rejecting globalisation and being considered a refusenik state. While Brexit had many origins, such as from fear of immigration, it also showcased a new class war between newocracy (the people who benefit from globalisation) and the people left behind, with the people being left behind winning the vote and rejecting globalisation.

- We are seeing people losing their jobs due to the forces of technology and globalisation but struggling to find new jobs. In 2010, only two per cent of Americans worked in agriculture, 20 per cent worked in industry and 78 per cent worked as teachers, doctors, webpage designers and so forth in the service industry. When jobs are continually disrupted by new technologies, people ask, what will the jobs of the future be?

- We are seeing young people struggling to deal with large student debts, struggling to save for a home and struggling to deal with insecure work.

- We are seeing people worrying about the rise of artificial intelligence, and there is a growing campaign to create intelligent assisting machines. According to Yuval Noah Harari, in his book Homo Deus: A Brief History of Tomorrow, 'Microsoft is developing Cortana which is an AI personal assistant which Microsoft hopes to include as an integral feature of future versions of Windows. Users will be encouraged to allow Cortana access to all their files, emails and applications, so that it will get to know them, and can offer its advice on myriad matters, as well as becoming a virtual agent representing the user's interests...Microsoft's Cortana is not alone in this game. Google Now and Apple's Siri are headed in the same direction.'[21]

- We are seeing a range of new global corporations, such as Uber, Netflix, Amazon, Alibaba, and Airbnb, emerge that aim to provide greater convenience to people yet fail to fully pay taxes in each country they operate in and adhere to local regulations. It is vital that a new set of global governance is created to fully regulate these global corporations. According to Michael J. Sandel, 'A century ago, we found ways to rein in the unaccountable power associated with the Industrial Revolution. Today, we need to figure out how to rein in the unaccountable power associated with the digital revolution.'[22]

- We are seeing nation states, like the UN and EU, struggling to deal with the growing World of Disorder that is emerging, and, as a result, people are losing faith in democracy. We are also seeing nation states and different organisations undermining democratic elections through hacking. We are experiencing an increase in fake news that is undermining democracy and elections around the world.

- We are also seeing people losing trust in important institutions such as governments, the media and religious organisations.

- We are experiencing a rise in nationalism and authoritarianism that is a critical part of the forces of technology and globalisation, as evidenced by the Brexit vote and the election of US President Donald Trump.

- As a result of this growing World of Disorder, we must aim to rise above these challenges and counter them by bringing the world together for the common good.

CHAPTER 3: GLOBAL CITIZENSHIP

In order to create a globalised society, or a Republic Earth, we need individuals, nation states and corporations to obey four sets of civic responsibilities to build a new common global agenda. Citizenship is an extremely important principle, and as we create a principle of global citizenship, it is vital that individuals, nation states and corporations obey this principle.

The first set of civic responsibilities as global citizens is to appreciate the magnificence of our blue-green planet. We must all try to protect Mother Earth, especially for future generations. Humanity has lost its connection with nature via advances in technology, and we must reconnect with nature and protect it. We must promote planetary care and avoid desecrating the Earth, as the growing World of Disorder has the ability to threaten the future of humanity itself.

The second set of civic responsibilities of global citizenship is to obey two foundational principles of democracy and the republic. Globally, 167 countries classify themselves as democratic, and 135 countries classify themselves as a republic; so both principles are universally acceptable.[23] In the 21st century we need individuals, nation states and corporations to fully embrace the principles of democracy and the republic. We need to ensure that all 7.7 billion people are able to have their democratic voice heard, so if someone is finding it difficult to adjust to the transition to a global society, they are free to speak out and seek assistance.

Over recent years I have been working closely with the taxi and hire car industry in Australia, which has had its business model disrupted by the forces of technology and globalisation, triggering the rise of companies such as Uber. In terms of the taxi and hire car industry, we should not be condemning them for failing to transition to a globalised society, but rather try to assist them to update their technology and to go global in the 21st century. The industry is currently protesting in Australia because they feel no one is listening to their concerns, and they have every right to democratically raise their concerns. This is only one example as there are many other similar cases around the world. Now it is up to governments to act to address the democratic concerns of those affected by the forces of technology and globalisation so that people can succeed in the transition to a globalised society.

We also need to create a new republican culture where power is always in the hands of the people, and that each person, nation state and corporation is just as important as everyone else. We must understand that we are all equal, no matter where we live around the world. There are no 'chosen people' in Republic Earth, as we are all chosen people. We also want to break down tyrannical and authoritarian structures, and create a republican culture of fairness and equality so that all people can benefit from the opportunities of a globalised society.

The third set of civic responsibilities of global citizenship is to obey the two principles of security and opportunity. For a globalised society to succeed, we need individuals, nation states and corporations to feel secure so that they can access all the opportunities that a globalised society has to offer. Strengthening job security, health security, educational security, energy security and community/national/inter-national security will allow people to access new job opportunities, health opportunities and educational opportunities. Security and opportunity are two core principles for a Republic Earth society to succeed.

Personally, I believe the Australian Labor Party and its values of standing up for workers' rights, a minimum wage, a decent education and having access to healthcare are fast becoming universal values that can help create a fair, just and equal globalised society. Accordingly, I believe the Australian Labor Party can play a major role in helping to create the policies, principles and structures for a globalised society to succeed in the 21st century.

The fourth set of civic responsibilities is to obey and embrace the four essential human freedoms, as outlined by former US President Franklin D. Roosevelt in 1941:[24]

1. Freedom of speech: everybody's democratic voice must be heard in a globalised society, provided they do no harm to others.

2. Freedom of religion: allow every person to worship their own faith in their own way, provided they do no harm to others.

3. Freedom from want: translated into world terms means ensuring that all citizens are provided with a social safety net or social security so that if they lose their jobs or something goes wrong in their lives, there will be a basic level of financial support to assist them.

4. Freedom from fear: we need to ensure that every person feels safe and secure in their own community and is provided with a sense of national and global security for a globalised society to succeed.

Humans are always looking forward to something bigger and better; becoming citizens of Republic Earth can become that exciting new experience for the 21st century. Although the success of creating a brand-new globalised society is not guaranteed, if we keep the faith and work together, we can bring the world together for the common good.

Interestingly, at the time the world is coming together to form a globalised society or a Republic Earth, humans are on the verge of having the ability to leave our planet and head to another planet—Mars. Before we head to Mars, however, I believe we must work to create a successful globalised society where we heal this planet from the adverse effects of climate change, deal with economic inequality and create a fairer society, and work to civilise new technologies so that they benefit humanity. If we succeed, it will be a powerful statement for humanity that we can come together for the common good and create a Republic Earth.

CHAPTER 4: GLOBAL BATTLE: WORLD OF ORDER VS WORLD OF DISORDER

As mentioned earlier, if a globalised society or a Republic Earth is going to succeed, we must successfully grow the new **World of Order**, which means to grow the:

- global middle class and jobs;

- renewable energy economy;

- digital revolution;

- gender equality and wave of transparency;

- medical breakthroughs that are seeing people live longer with better health outcomes;

- global governance structures;

- Republic Earth—liberal, democratic World of Order.

However, we have two major threats to the emergence of a global society and new World of Order. First, we must successfully address the key global challenges in the new **World of Disorder**, which are leading to an increase in:

- climate change threats;

- inequality;

- terrorism and cyberterrorism;

- displaced people and refugees;

- harm caused by the digital revolution and artificial intelligence, meaning we need to rein in the unaccountable power associated with the digital revolution;

- the threat posed by nuclear weapons;

- autocratic regimes that threaten democratic nations.

Second, we need to counter the challenges being posed by the auto-cratic governments of the People's Republic of China and the Russian Federation, which are using a new form of sharp power to take control away from democratic nations. Australia and other democratic nations must stand up to these autocratic threats, and not only begin a count-er-revolution against authoritarianism, but play hardball to ensure a democratic global society is achieved.

CHAPTER 5: REPUBLIC EARTH ORGANISATION—GLOBAL GOVERNANCE

This book argues that Australia can play a key role in uniting the world for the common good via this new political concept called Republic Earth. In the following two chapters it will be outlined how Australia can help build the new structures of global governance in the 21st century and play a role in addressing the key global challenges by creating a Republic Earth Organisation to replace the G7, as well as being the leading democratic organisation for nation states.

CHAPTER 6: AUSTRALIAN REPUBLIC—REPUBLIC EARTH

So, let's begin the journey and provide a new hope for Australia and the world. In 2014, in Melbourne, we began the journey of creating a Republic Earth, but in 2019 we will formally establish a Republic Earth Organisation to help grow our global society and address the key challenges we face.

Interestingly, in Australia we are beginning a new campaign for a transition to an Australian Republic. So as part of this campaign, we could also be the nation that inspires the creation of a Republic Earth and creates a globalised society. If the US became the first modern democracy when it became a republic in 1776, and India became the largest democratic nation when it officially became a republic in 1950, Australia could help to create a global democracy and a Republic Earth when it becomes a republic by 2025. Australia and multicultural cities like Melbourne have an important role to play in creating a globalised society, and so in 2019 the building of this new exciting **World of Order** will begin.

Let's provide a much-needed new hope for the world and build the world of tomorrow by aiming to create a globalised society or a Republic Earth in the 21st century. We have a choice: we can build bridges or we can build walls; we can go backward and isolate ourselves or move forward and interconnect in a new noble way. We are calling to those wanting to join Republic Earth. This is the beginning and we are looking for members to start a movement, a Republic Earth movement. Please visit www.republicearth.org to sign up if you wish to join and participate.

Now is the time for boldness, so let's create a Republic Earth.

PART 1

THE WORLD OF ORDER BATTLE IN THE 21ST CENTURY

Ω

We are currently experiencing an exciting transition to a global society; however, unbeknown to many people, we are also in a battle to set the rules for this new World of Order.

On the one hand, we have a group of countries committed to democratic values that aim to use English as the global language to create a robust global middle class and a successful global society. This democratic alliance includes international entities such as the Group of Seven Nations (G7), the European Union (EU), and the North Atlantic Treaty Organization (NATO). This book makes the argument that this group of democratic nations needs to create a new entity called the Republic Earth Organisation, or some other global institution, so as to create the new democratic rules-based order for the 21st century that will enable a global society to succeed.

The Republic Earth Organisation would be created by Australia and hopefully involve the following democratic member nations: USA, UK, Canada, New Zealand, Germany, France, Italy, Japan, South Korea, Indonesia, India, Albania, Belgium, Bulgaria, Croatia, Czech Republic, Denmark, Estonia, Greece, Hungary, Iceland, Kosovo, Latvia, Lithuania, Luxembourg, Montenegro, The Netherlands, Norway, Poland, Portugal, Romania, Slovenia, Spain, Switzerland, Mauritius, Malta, Uruguay, Cape Verde, Costa Rica, Chile, Botswana, Israel, Taiwan, Cyprus, Jamaica, South Africa, Timor-Leste, Panama, Trinidad and Tobago, Argentina, Brazil, Suriname, Ireland, Ghana, Colombia, Dominican Republic, Lesotho, Malaysia, Peru, Guyana, El Salvador, Mexico, Tunisia, Singapore,

Hong Kong, Namibia, Paraguay, Senegal, Papua New Guinea, Ecuador, Guatemala, Fiji, Honduras, Ukraine, Zambia, Mali, Benin, North Macedonia, Bolivia, Malawi, Tanzania, Bangladesh, Liberia, Kenya, Madagascar, Uganda, Bhutan, Morocco, Bosnia and Herzegovina, Burkina Faso, Lebanon, Sierra Leone, Nicaragua, Thailand, Palestine, Nigeria, Iraq, Gambia, Haiti, Mozambique and Ethiopia.

The goal of the Republic Earth Organisation is to have all nations as members; however, each nation will need to embrace democracy and celebrate democracy as one of humanity's finest achievements in order for the global society to succeed. The Republic Earth Organisation will also aim to create a security alliance with all member nations. From a security point of view, the main mission of the organisation is to fulfil former US President Roosevelt's goal of creating a united world or a United Nations.

In contrast we also have a group of primarily autocratic countries that are members of the Shanghai Cooperation Organization (SCO), or Shanghai Pact, which is a Eurasian political, economic and security organisation created in 2001 by the leaders of China, Russia, Kazakhstan, Kyrgyzstan, Tajikistan and Uzbekistan.[25] Under the SCO, the following countries are under the sphere of influence: Pakistan, Afghanistan, Belarus, Iran, Mongolia, Armenia, Azerbaijan, Cambodia, Nepal, India, Sri Lanka, Turkey, Turkmenistan, Moldova, and the Philippines.

In 2018, the Shanghai Pact was leading the way in promoting its global agenda and had enticed nations such as Iran and maybe now Pakistan to join their cause. Unfortunately, the democratic alliance of nations have yet to commit to a global agenda that unites the world for the common good because it is still beholden to 20th century institutions. As mentioned earlier, the democratic alliance needs to create a global institution, such as a Republic Earth Organisation, which entices nations to join their cause based on democratic values. In 2019, Australia should lead efforts to create this new democratic organisation that creates new governance structures, so that the exciting new global society can prosper.

It is important to point out that organisations such as the UN, ASEAN and the G20 are important multilateral organisations that provide an opportunity for nations to enter into dialogue on a whole range of global issues. However, organisations such as the UN will remain an independent organisation in the global battle to set the rules-based order for the World of Order or the global society. Despite the UN, we have yet to achieve the goal of uniting all nations under one global security pact. Hence, the battle now begins between the Republic Earth Organisation and the Shanghai Cooperation Organization to control and govern the new World of Order in the 21st century.

CHAPTER 7: REPUBLIC EARTH ORGANISATION

In 2014, the Republic Earth Organisation was founded in Australia to help create a global democracy in the 21st century and to celebrate democracy as humanity's finest achievement. The organisation has struggled to gain influence so far, but hopefully post the 2019 Australian Federal Election a new foreign policy agenda for Australia can be created within the Australian Labor Party, which would include the formal creation of the Republic Earth Organisation.

Australia, the US and Japan joined forces in 2018 to counter the growing influence of China in the Indo-Pacific region, which was seen as a step towards reviving the Quadrilateral Security Dialogue (QSD/Quad) that began in 2007 with member states Australia, India, Japan and the US, aiming to establish an 'Asian Arc of Democracy'.[26] However, the QSD has not succeeded insofar as India must be a vital member. A more ambitious democratic alliance needs to be created to counter the growing autocratic threat posed by the ambitions of the SCO.

We argue that the Republic Earth Organisation would be better placed to not only set the rules-based order for the 21st century, but would also be better placed to tackle the key global challenges emerging in the growing World of Disorder.

The Republic Earth Organisation is not an anti-China and anti-Russian organisation, and fully embraces the Chinese and Russian peoples, cultures and languages. However, the democratic Republic Earth Organisation is concerned with the global agenda put forward by the autocratic SCO, which is led by China and Russia. One must remember that Sun Yat-sen founded a democratic Republic of China in 1912, and Mikhail Gorbachev brought about democratic changes to Russia in 1989 that led to democratic elections in 1991, and thus the Republic Earth Organisation hopes that both China and Russia could return to fully embracing democracy.

At the end of the Cold War the world came so close to creating a democratically united world or a United Nations. Under Mikhail Gorbachev leadership Russia became a democracy and the people of China were demanding democratic change. To hold back this growing spirit of democracy and global democracy the Chinese Government in 1989 decided to shoot its own people in one of the greatest atrocities of the 20th Century (In 2019 protests in Hong Kong and Taiwan will mark the 30th Anniversary of this massacre, which will also promote the virtues of democracy towards mainland China). In addition, post 1991 Gorbachev's newly formed democracy in Russia was destroyed and replaced by the Autocratic rule of Boris Yeltsin and now Vladimir Putin. We had a chance to unite the world but the Chinese Government and the Russian Government remain committed to form a new global agenda that is autocratic and not democratic.

In the 20th century, one of the great achievements of former US President Roosevelt was that he defended democracy against fascism. By 1941 there were only 11 democracies, and President Roosevelt worried that it might not be possible to shield 'the great flame of democracy from the blackout of barbarism'.[27] In this hour of weakness for democracy, President Roosevelt showed tremendous leadership during World War II and ensured that democracy survived and prospered.

After World War II, a community of democracies emerged that came to be known as 'the West', and eventually spread to include democracies around the world, such as Japan, Brazil, South Korea, Indonesia and India. At the core of this community were two pillars: the US and the group of European democracies that became the European Union.

According to Thomas Friedman, '"The West" was not just a state of mind. It was an association of countries with shared interests, institutions and values — particularly the values of liberty, democracy, free markets and the rule of law — which made the post-World War II world, though far from perfect, a steadily more prosperous, free and decent place for more and more people. This community of democracies was also a beacon, a refuge and a magnet for those who wanted to embrace its values but were denied them where they lived.'[28]

Unfortunately, in the 21st century the community of democracies has never been under more assault by the threats posed by the growing World of Disorder. In 2016, it is understood that foreign influence by autocratic regimes affected the result of the US presidential election and the UK European Union Membership Referendum.[29] We are also witnessing autocratic regimes using a new form of sharp power to influence democratic nations all around the world, while climate change and conflicts have led to an increase in the number of displaced people and refugees, forcing more pressure on democratic nations wishing to assist. For example, according to Thomas Friedman, 'Toppling Qaddafi [in Libya] without building a new order may go down as the single dumbest action the NATO alliance ever took. It took the lid off Africa, leading to some 600,000 asylum seekers and illegal migrants flocking to Italy's shores in recent years, with 300,000 staying there and the rest filtering into other E.U. countries. This has created wrangles within the bloc over who should absorb how many migrants and has spawned nationalist-populist backlashes in almost every E.U. country.'[30]

According to the UN, the total population of Europe is 740 million and Africa is 1.2 billion, but by 2050, Europe will shrink to 700 million and Africa will double to 2.4 billion.[31] Hence, if democratic nations fail to address the increase in displaced people and refugees now, then the problem could get much worse in the coming years.

Since World War II, the US working with European nations has led the community of democracies to make the world steadily freer, more stable and more prosperous. Unfortunately, US President Donald Trump has little appreciation of the EU-US partnership and has failed to show any form of global leadership. Meanwhile, according to the World Bank, economic output in the Eurozone was lower in 2017 than in 2009, while in China it grew 139 per cent.[32] It is clear that Donald Trump is missing in action in the battle to control the new World of Order. One might say he is trying to reduce the threat of nuclear weapons by meeting with the Marshal of North Korea, Kim Jong-un, on 12 June 2018.[33] However, since the summit it has been reported that North Korea has expanded ballistic missile production, which is a disturbing trend, and thus Donald Trump may actually have made things worse.[34]

Moreover, according to Thomas Friedman, in terms of the US-EU relationship, 'Trump actually pressed British Prime Minister Theresa May to make a sharp Brexit from the E.U., if she wanted to have a free-trade agreement with the U.S., and he characterized the E.U. not as a partner on trade but as a "foe." Trump seems to prefer that the E.U. fracture so he can try to strike better trade deals with the countries individually. This is such foolish talk. It was the U.S. and what became the E.U. that took the lead in not only repelling communism but in shaping the rules and catalysing institutions that managed the key global issues after WWII — like trade, migration, environment and human rights — helping more people around the globe grow out of poverty faster than ever before.'[35]

It is important to understand that the change in the pace of change regarding the climate, globalisation and technology has thrown up a whole new set of challenges very fast—extreme weather, cybercrime, crypto-currencies, social networks, deepfake technologies, self-driving vehicles, artificial intelligence, biological design tools and questions of how to distinguish among refugees, economic migrants and asylum seekers. These can be managed only through global cooperation and new rules.

In light of the US (under Donald Trump) withdrawing from its global leadership responsibility (Trump has pulled out of the Paris Agreement of 2015, the Trans-Pacific Partnership of 2016, the UN Human Rights Council and threatened to pull out of NATO and the WTO), and that the UK is struggling to agree to a deal to leave the European Union, it is vital for a democratic nation like Australia to step forward and lead efforts to protect the community of democracies.[36] Trump appears to be more interested in meeting autocratic leaders like Kim Jong-un rather than promoting democracy around the world. Accordingly, Australia should lead efforts to create a Republic Earth Organisation that aims to set the global rules or norms for the 21st century.

Australia should seek to work with the US, the EU, G7 nations and democratic nations around the world to build an alliance to counter the agenda put forward by the autocratic SCO. It is true that French President Emmanuel Macron is trying to make sense of the 21st century and wants to take a leading role in addressing global challenges and restoring pride in the European Union. In his speech to the Seventy-third United Nations General Assembly, Macron wished to use his presidency of the G7 Nations in 2019 to promote a third way of building a new rules-based order.[37]

Macron should also be congratulated for hosting a Paris Peace Forum on 11 November 2018 to redouble efforts for global peace. However, it is unfortunate that Macron does not believe in 'one great globalized people'.[38] Hopefully in ongoing discussions with the French President we can encourage him to appreciate that the third way that he is building should include the creation of a Republic Earth. In his last year as US President in 2016, Barack Obama took a global outlook and met with many young people from around the world. Obama understood that a brand-new global society was emerging, and thus it is now up to current democratic political leaders like Australia to embrace this global society and ensure that this new World of Order prospers and a global democratic society is achieved. Unfortunately, in the 21st century the SCO has been leading efforts to provide global leadership as Western democratic nations have been distracted, but democratic nations can now come together to create a Republic Earth Organisation to provide global leadership.

CHAPTER 8: THE SHANGHAI COOPERATION ORGANIZATION (SCO)

The SCO was created on 15 June 2001 in Shanghai, China, by the leaders of China, Kazakhstan, Kyrgyzstan, Russia, Tajikistan, and Uzbekistan.[39] The principal leaders of the SCO are China and Russia, but, interestingly, India and Pakistan joined SCO as full members on 9 June 2017 at a summit in Astana, Kazakhstan.[40]

We understand that in both China and Russia they wish to restore their supremacy on the world stage. In China it has often been claimed that they endured a 'Century of Humiliation', which describes the period from the mid-19th to mid-20th centuries, when China was diplomatically and militarily dominated by Western colonial powers. Ending at the close of the Chinese Civil War and the establishment of the People's Republic of China, the period remains a major component of 'modern China's founding narrative'.[41] Under the leadership of the Chinese Communist Party (CCP), China's overriding national goal now is righting the injustice of the century of humiliation by achieving 'the great rejuvenation of the Chinese nation'.[42] Since he entered office, authoritarian President Xi Jinping has widely promoted the 'Chinese Dream' of achieving rejuvenation.[43] Called *fuxing* in Chinese, this rejuvenation is an end state in which China has overcome the humiliating handicaps of colonial history and has become strong and powerful enough to prevent its recurrence.[44]

To China's credit, the 'Chinese Dream' is being achieved, as according to Australia's most recent Foreign Policy White Paper, it projects GDP on purchasing power parity out to 2030. US GDP rises from US $18.6 trillion in 2016 to US $24 trillion by 2030. China's GDP rises from US $21.4 trillion to US $42.4 trillion over the same period.[45] So within a decade, the Chinese economy is set to become nearly twice as large as the economies of the US, India ($20.9 trillion) and the EU ($23.3 trillion) and seven times larger than the economy of Japan.[46]

The trajectory outlined by these economic figures represents a fundamental reshaping of the global and regional economy. It is a reshaping with profound implications for the region and for the US. Meanwhile, the 2017 PWC report *The World in 2050* projects the four largest economies will be China, India, US and Indonesia, in that order.[47] So by mid-century, Australians are likely to live in a world where the four largest economies are all Indo-Pacific powers.

In Russia it is often claimed that they were humiliated after losing the Cold War and the key battle of the 20th century between capitalism and communism. However, since 2000, Vladimir Putin, as President and Prime Minister of the Russian Federation, has sought to restore Russia's place on the world stage.

On the one hand, we welcome both China and Russia's attempts to put forward an alternative vision for a new rules-based order for the 21st century. However, both nations are autocratic regimes that rather than using soft power to entice nations to their visions, are using a new form of sharp power (Sharp power is the use of manipulative diplomatic policies by one country to influence and undermine the political system of a target country) that is deeply troubling for democratic nations like Australia.[48] At present, both China and Russia are currently acting like bullies on a global scale and are covertly trying to take power away from all nations around the world.

One of the chief concerns is that the government of the People's Republic of China and the government of the Russian Federation, as the two key principal members of the Shanghai Pact, have, as autocratic regimes, spent billions of dollars shaping public opinion and perceptions around the world.[49]

Autocratic regimes such as China and Russia are employing a diverse toolkit that includes thousands of people-to-people exchanges, wide-ranging cultural activities, education programs, and the development of media enterprises and information initiatives with global reach.

According to the National Endowment of Democracy's Sharp Power Report, 'this authoritarian or foreign influence is not principally about attraction or even persuasion; instead, it centers on distraction and manipulation. These ambitious authoritarian regimes, which systematically suppress political pluralism and free expression at home, are increasingly seeking to apply similar principles internationally to secure their interests.'[50]

Moreover, in terms of sheer numbers, President Jinping it has been claimed is arguably one of the most accomplished human rights violators alive today. Jinping's CCP governs 18 per cent of humankind, depriving them of freedom of speech, political rights, religious freedom, independent media and open internet access—all of which should be fundamental components of modern society.[51] Political indoctrination is being reinserted into Chinese curricula, and an Orwellian 'social credit' system is being developed to more closely control individuals' every behaviour.[52] Additionally, the CCP continues its efforts to wipe out the ethnic heritage of Tibetans and Uighurs, with recent reports confirming the existence of massive internment camps in Xinjiag province.

In addition, President Jinping regularly promotes the 'Belt and Road Initiative'—a massive westward infrastructure program—as a 'win-win' undertaking that will fill infrastructure gaps in less-developed countries for mutual profit.[53] But major components of the Belt and Road have proven to be debt traps that endanger participants' sovereignty and increase China's political influence, while benefiting corrupt officials and bringing few opportunities to the average citizen. In some places, like Sri Lanka, the Maldives and Pakistan, it's also apparent that the Belt and Road is a cover for military expansion.[54]

According to Brendon Hong, China's 'strategy is based, significantly, on a favorite European colonial strategy of the 19th century, when debts and debt collection was used around the world to gain decisive influence on weaker countries'.[55]

Today, Beijing's expanding influence as a global creditor can be seen in some striking figures: 'As of June last year, 44 percent of Burma's external debt was owned by China. Laos, which often is characterized as the poorest country in this corner of Asia, has kept the details of its major projects under wraps, but reportedly has received loans of $465 million and $600 million from the Export-Import Bank of China, meant as operation costs for the China-Laos Railway and funds to cover a hydropower project.'[56]

According to Brendon Hong, 'Move west, and we find Sri Lanka, which is obligated to pay China $480 million in interest each year. The strain on Colombo has been so great that a 70-percent share of the island nation's Hambantota Port was handed over to a Chinese state-owned firm on a 99-year lease. Further afoot, more than 70 percent of the Maldives' external debt is owed to China.'[57]

'On the African continent, China now owns 70 percent of Kenya's foreign debt, a tenfold increase in five years. Its neighbor Djibouti has made headlines for hosting the first overseas facility of the People's Liberation Army; more profound is the fact that China had loaned $1.4 billion to the East African nation as of last year, a figure that represents 75 percent of Djibouti's GDP.'[58]

'Most importantly for the United States, the People's Republic owns 19 percent of all American Treasury Bills, notes, and bonds held by foreign bodies as of May 2018 ... The United States aside, Beijing offers easy loans to nations eager to modernize their infrastructure, often in places where there is a crucial need for such improvements. It is common for allegations of collusion between local government officials and Chinese entities to arise, but this hasn't slowed down the deal making. Chinese money goes to a new metro in Lahore, a bridge over the Padma River in Bangladesh, airport upgrades in Harare, a new nuclear power plant somewhere in Turkey, and a litany of other projects. For those in the non-aligned "Third World," it is China's coffers that seem to offer a potential path to prosperity.'[59]

According to Brendon Hong, one key area is to 'look to Pakistan, where a gem of the Belt and Road Initiative is located. The China-Pakistan Economic Corridor (CPEC) is a $62 billion project that encompasses a deep water port in Gwadar, roadway projects, new railroads, energy sector constructions, and cooperation in agriculture and technology fields. In theory, the CPEC will bolster the Pakistani economy and allow

China to access the Indian Ocean (which is of major interest to the Chinese navy).'[60]

As a world leader, the United States will not be displaced for years to come, but the erosion of American influence is fact, exacerbated by chaos in the current administration. The Trump Administration is currently missing in action to the current threat posed by the SCO.

Moreover, from the Obama administration's 'pivot' to Asia, to the US withdrawal from the Trans-Pacific Partnership; from regular military drills with South Korea, to the presence of American military bases and troops in East and Southeast Asia, China's policymakers see America's actions in the past decades as a grand attempt to restrict the rise of the party and the Chinese nation, but that containment has never worked. Instead, the foundations for a new world order have been laid.[61]

In 2018, Xi returned to Beijing after a visit to four African countries over 10 days—his fourth trip to the continent since becoming president.[62] During a stop in Johannesburg, he called for BRICS (Brazil, Russia, India, China and South Africa) to unfurl a second 'golden decade' of cooperation.[63] After the photo ops, commentators noted that Donald Trump has not visited the continent, and doesn't seem to have plans to. With smaller, often indebted countries falling in line with China's geopolitical agenda, and BRICS nations securing regional power, the Chinese empire is set to be globe-spanning, robust and impossible to hold back. For example, more than 2,500 Chinese peacekeeping personnel are already stationed in countries such as South Sudan, Liberia and Mali.[64]

Meanwhile, in 2018 President Vladimir Putin sought to forge closer ties with the US. According to Thomas Friedman, 'There are other parallels between Trumpism and Putism: the glorification of oil, gas, and mining over science and technology; the elevation of white, Christian, nationalist values; and the neutering of the legislative branch — today's G.O.P.-dominated Congress behaves just like the rubber stamp Russian Duma. Worse, this Russification of politics is also spreading — to the Philippines, Turkey, Hungary, Poland and maybe soon to Brazil. A few more years of this Russification of America and the rot will be everywhere.'[65]

Moreover, in September 2018, Russia hosted a massive military exercise combined with China and Mongolia to showcase the growing military power of the SCO. Both President Putin and President Jinping know that they have a small window over the next decade to maximise their control over the world. Hence, Russia and China are building their military capabilities to ensure the SCO will set the rules in the 21st century.

One of the best analysis comes from Dr Christopher Ashley Ford, Assistant Secretary, Bureau of International Security and Nonproliferation, who states that, 'Indeed, with remarkable candor, Chinese leaders of no lesser a stature than Xi Jinping himself have made clear that the Communist Chinese Party-State now sees itself as the paladin of a distinct ideology — a socio-political "operating system," if you will, characterized by market-oriented state capitalism steered by an authoritarian Leninist party organization — that is in a long-term struggle with democratic capitalism as the dominant model for the 21st-Century. At the 19th Party Congress, Xi Jinping famously declared that China's emergence as a great power demonstrates a new path and governance model for modernization."

'Open talk of a so-called "China model" of development that began to be much more prevalent in Chinese writings after the 2008 financial crash has thus now explicitly blossomed under Xi Jinping into a full-blown concept of competition between systems to decide the geopolitical future of the world. I guess you could call Xi's approach "Cold War with Chinese characteristics."

'So China's ambitions are huge. Chinese strategic writings make clear that the objective of the CCP's strategy is not merely to acquire power and influence for China on the world stage, but in fact to *displace* U.S. power and influence so as to reclaim the central geopolitical status and role of which China believes it was robbed by Western imperialism.'[66]

In the end, it is important to understand that China, not Russia, leads the Shanghai Cooperation Organization, and President Jinping's leadership seeks to advance China's interests, not within the prevailing global order, but at its expense. For now, it is working. China has no peer competitors at present to be concerned about and plenty of cash to advance its interests in other parts of the world. But in making himself into an emperor, Jinping has ensured that the world will come to realise he has no clothes. His totalitarianism inside China is severe, and China's international conduct is drastically out of step with global norms. The key is for the world to refuse to accept it any longer. President Jinping's egregious conduct is likely to alienate China from the rest of the world, and nations like Australia must raise our concerns. We must fight back and create a **counter-revolution against authoritarianism**, and play **hardball** to curtail one of the major threats to global stability.

In light of this emerging threat to democratic nations around the world, we definitely need to create a Republic Earth Organisation to counter this threat in order to keep democratic nations like Australia safe, as well as to promote democratic values and create a proper rules-based order so that global society can succeed.

CHAPTER 9: GLOBAL ECONOMY
and GROWING MIDDLE CLASS

In the 21st century we are witnessing an astonishing increase in the global middle class. Most people live in one of 600 cities, with better job outcomes and education outcomes than previously. Homi Kharas, an expert on the global middle class, estimated in a recent study that 3.2 billion people, or 42 per cent of the total world population, are now in the global middle class.[67] This group's size increases by 160 million people per year, and assuming current rates of growth, in a few years most of humanity will live, for the first time in history, in middle-class homes or better.[68]

To make the point even clearer, the World Bank states that, 'in 2015, 10 percent of the world's population lived on less than US$1.90 a day, compared to 11 percent in 2013. That's down from nearly 36 percent in 1990'.[69]

The key architect of this success story was former US President Franklin D. Roosevelt. In a time of great danger, Roosevelt embraced experimentation, trying whatever he could to get the US out of the Great Depression. In simple terms, Roosevelt passed laws to make capitalism safer and avoid the boom and bust economic cycle. Roosevelt made it safer to put money into banks, he separated ordinary banking from Wall Street speculation and put a cop on the beat on Wall Street. Such reforms made a real difference but ensured capitalism survived in America, and ensured that capitalism rather than communism was the best way to lift people out of poverty and into the middle class. Both China and Russia need to understand that capitalism, not communism, has lifted millions of their citizens out of poverty and into the global middle class.

The key issue now is that people in Western nations like Australia, the US and England feel that the middle class is under threat, as families deal with a lack of wage growth and rising expenses. The Republic Earth Organisation not only wants to work on ideas to continue to increase the global middle class but also to better protect working people, who, once they join or have been in the middle class for decades, don't start to struggle financially due to a lack of wage growth or rising expenses.

In August 2018, US Senator Elizabeth Warren led efforts to not only better protect the US middle class by proposing a new Federal Bill called the Accountable Capitalism Act, but was also better protecting the global middle class.[70] The aim of the bill is to redistribute trillions of dollars from rich executives and shareholders to the middle class without costing a dollar. The Republic Earth Organisation would aim to encourage member nations to pass similar bills in their own nations. We want all peoples and all nations to enjoy the benefits of the global middle class. However, the SCO does not mind if the middle class disappears in the US, the UK, in EU nations or Australia, as this would only benefit China and Russia.

The Republic Earth Organisation fully understands that we now live in a global economy and we cannot let the middle class be undermined in any nation. An economic crisis in one nation now affects all nations. Hence, the Republic Earth Organisation will continue to work on a daily basis to grow and protect the global middle class in the 21st century.

One area of concern for the global society is young people. Young people will enjoy the benefits of the increase in the global middle class but many struggle currently with the costs of education and not being able to find employment. Even if young people find a job, many now cannot meet living expenses or afford to save for a loan to purchase a house. As an older millennial, I can relate with the concerns of young people, and I truly love their spirit to travel and engage with the world. What the Republic Earth Organisation truly appreciates is that young people today are the first generation of human citizens who have an international outlook. Ask most young people and you can see that they love to travel, listen to music from around the world and eat global cuisine. One of the most popular places for young people to travel to is Bali in Indonesia as it is affordable. The Republic Earth Organisation wishes to work on new policies to make it easier and more affordable for young people to become educated and find employment, as well as being able to enjoy what the world has to offer and have fun.

The global economy over recent years has increased the global middle class, and global growth is projected to reach 3.9 per cent in 2018 and 2019 when all the numbers are in, according to the International Monetary Fund.[71] The US had two strong quarters of economic growth in 2018, and China, despite a slowdown, is continuing to grow at 6.6 per cent.[72] However, the economic data for the third quarter of 2018 showed a marked slowdown in the growth of the Eurozone, while others worry about an ongoing trade war between China and the US undermining the global economy, while others worry about recessions in nations.[73] Nouriel Roubini, who foresaw the global financial crisis, is one who believes the US may be heading for a recession in 2020.[74] While others are worried about the rising burden of public and private debt in China, which could yet undermine financial stability.[75]

The Economist believes key global economic risks include: 'a US-China trade conflict morphs into a full-blown global trade war; US Corporate debt burden turns downturn into a recession; China suffers a disorderly and prolonged economic downturn; political gridlock leads to a disorderly no deal Brexit'.[76] The world's economic future remains uncertain, and recent growth figures are promising, but creating a new Global Economic and Trade Organisation could help nations work closely together and avoid some of the looming pitfalls that could undermine the growing global economy and growing middle class.

One of the major threats to the global economy and the stability of the middle class is economic inequality. Too much is still in the hands of the few, and more needs to be done to properly tax the rich and ensure a fairer global society is created. This issue of economic inequality will be discussed later in this book, as economic inequality is one of the key global challenges that needs to be addressed in the growing World of Disorder.

The Republic Earth Organisation believes we must do all we can as democratic nations to continue to ensure the global economy works for all citizens around the world, and that we continue to grow the global middle class and ensure that all people can be members of it and enjoy a great quality of life in the 21st century. This will ensure the new World of Order and global society can succeed.

CHAPTER 10: GROWING THE RENEWABLE ENERGY ECONOMY

We have recently seen an exciting growth in the renewable energy economy to counter the devastating effects of climate change. Many nations, like the US and Australia, however, are still struggling to move their national policy away from a pro fossil fuel energy system to a renewable energy system. But if you wish to achieve lower energy costs and a cleaner environment, then all nations will have to embrace the renewable energy economy at some point.

The Republic Earth Organisation wishes to work with member nations to grow the renewable energy economy around the world, so that by the end of the 21st century we are powering all the world's energy needs via renewable energy. To achieve this goal, we need to embrace what Energy Innovation CEO Hal Harvey calls the four zeros:

1. Zero carbon grid.

2. Zero emission vehicles.

3. Zero net energy buildings.

4. Zero waste manufacturing.[77]

Around the world there are growing calls for action to invest in a renewable energy economy. Despite the fact that the Trump Administration is still in favour of the fossil fuel industry, there are growing calls in the US for a Green New Deal. Inspired by former US President Roosevelt's New Deal of the 1930s to tackle the Great Depression and grow the American middle class, the promise of a Green New Deal advanced by newly elected US Congresswoman Alexandria Ocasio-Cortez, and now backed by over 14 other representatives, is growing in momentum.[78]

The inspiration for the Green New Deal has come from two key activists: Bill McKibben, founder of 350.org, and Naomi Klein. Both understand, according to Naomi Klein, that, 'global emissions continue to rise, alongside average temperatures, with large swathes of the planet buffeted by record-breaking storms and scorched by unprecedented fires. The scientists convened in the Intergovernmental Panel on Climate Change have confirmed precisely what African and low lying island states have long since warned; that allowing temperatures to rise by 2 per cent is a death sentence, and only a 1.5 degree target gives us a fighting chance'.[79]

Despite the actions of current regimes in the US under a Trump Administration and in Australia under a Morrison Government to protect the fossil fuel industry, both Klein and McKibben feel more optimistic about our collective chances of averting climate breakdown because there is growing calls around the world to take action to get to a place in the 21st century, 'in which the worst climate outcomes are avoided and a new social compact is forged that is radically more humane than anything currently on offer'.[80]

The Republic Earth Organisation wants to build on this momentum in the US for a Green New Deal and actually put forward the need for democratic nations to unite to form a Global Planetary and Renewable Energy Organisation so as to ensure all the world's energy is produced by renewable energy as soon as possible this century.

In terms of the SCO, its leading nation, China, is committed to taking action against climate change and to building a renewable energy economy, whereas Russia and many other member nations are still in favour of maintaining a fossil fuel industry. In contrast, developed democratic nations are continuing to transition to renewable energy economies. Denmark, for example, is expected to generate 69 per cent of its energy from renewable sources by 2022, making it the world leader.[81] Ireland is second, with the International Energy Agency (IEA) Renewables report, and will generate more than one-third of its energy needs from renewable sources within four years.[82] In other European countries, including Spain, Germany and the UK, the share of wind and solar will exceed 25 per cent of total generation.[83]

The Republic Earth Organisation wants democratic nations to not only unite to accelerate the process towards permanently producing 100 per cent renewable energy in democratic developed nations, but also assist developing nations, especially nations like India, to accelerate their process towards renewable energy. In India, renewable capacity is expected to more than double by 2022. Solar and wind represent 90 per cent of India's capacity growth.[84] Accordingly, the Republic Earth Organisation believes leading democratic nations can play a role in assisting developing nations to transition to a renewable energy economy. Australia is perfectly placed to lead efforts to encourage all countries to transition to renewable energy. We have an abundance in renewable energy as wind and solar power is growing rapidly, and having previously been one of the great fossil fuel producers in the world, we can show countries how to transition away from fossil fuels and become a leading renewable energy economy instead.

The Republic Earth Organisation believes that most citizens of the world want governments to transition to renewable energy because it not only reduces family energy costs to eventually zero, but it also better protects our environment and Mother Earth. The world of tomorrow embraces renewable energy where families can take out a loan to purchase a renewable energy system at a low cost and then no longer have to pay energy costs as the renewable energy costs reduce to zero. This means that people will still have to purchase a car or an energy system, but will no longer have to pay for fuel or energy in their homes. This is a huge cost saving for family budgets. The renewable energy revolution will not only better protect our environment but actually make our global middle class stronger, as it will reduce cost of living pressures, giving our middle class more room to spend their precious money on other areas and not on purchasing fuel and energy.

We believe that creating a Global Planetary and Renewable Energy Organisation, as explained later in this book, will give the world the best chance to build a global renewable energy economy where 100 per cent of energy is permanently produced by renewable sources. We hope more citizens around the world will call for action to transition to renewable energy.

CHAPTER 11: DIGITAL REVOLUTION

This century, the digital revolution has allowed global society to grow and become interconnected. In 2018, 4.2 billion people out of 7.7 billion people were using the internet.[85] This means that over 50 per cent of the world's population is connected to the internet and enjoying the benefits of being interconnected. Experts believe that within 12 to 15 years, i.e. by 2030, the whole world's population will be globally connected, which is an amazing achievement and allows for a global society or a Republic Earth to be totally interconnected for the first time in history.

In light of the global society becoming interconnected via the digital revolution, the SCO and its leading member nations, China and Russia, have created a mission to become leaders in technology and seek ways to control the digital revolution. The Republic Earth Organisation believes that the SCO should not be able to gain control of the digital revolution as this would greatly harm our growing global democratic society. Countries like China have already created a social credit system to monitor its citizens online, which infringes their democratic human rights. If the SCO was able to gain control of the digital revolution, then we had better get ready for an Orwellian-style global social credit system to be rolled out, which will monitor every citizen around the world.[86]

The Republic Earth Organisation believes the digital revolution should remain democratic and that people's digital human rights of privacy should be protected. We welcome new technology companies into the global marketplace from countries like China and Russia; however, if they are seeking to use sharp power to gain control of the digital revolution, then democratic countries need to speak out and resist such attempts by companies seeking to do the bidding of the SCO. According to the Australian Foreign Investment Review Board, in many ways there are no private companies in China and they will do what they are told by the Chinese Government.[87]

Whether we like it or not, we are in a battle and the Republic Earth Organisation believes that democratic nations need to unite to better regulate the digital revolution and ensure it remains democratic and that people's human rights are protected.

The digital revolution has a long history, but in 1947, after World War II, the transistor was invented, which is the data transfer device that underpins digital technology.[88] In 1951, the first commercially available computer was released. In 1971, the first email was sent.[89] In 1989, Tim Berners Lee invented the World Wide Web whilst working at CERN.[90] In 2003, Skype was launched, in 2004, Facebook launched, in 2005, YouTube launched and in 2007, the iPhone was launched.[91] As an older millennial it has been amazing to witness the radical pace of change from the 1990s to now, and to see how quickly the digital revolution has developed. Now we are living in the information age. From healthcare to education, technology has transformed our lives, and the digital revolution shows no sign of slowing down, especially with virtual reality and artificial intelligence on the rise.

In 2018, the largest tech companies were: 1) Apple, US; 2) Amazon, US; 3) Alphabet (Google), US; Microsoft, US; 5) Samsung, South Korea; 6) Cisco, US; 7) Intel, US; 8) IBM, US; 9) Foxconn, Taiwan; 10) Sony, Japan; 11) Panasonic, Japan; 12) Hitachi, Japan; 13) Huawei, China.[92] In 2018, the following companies have been in existence for: Snapchat, 7 years; Uber, 9; Twitter, 12; Facebook, 14; Tesla, 15; Google, 20; Netflix, 21; Amazon, 24; Apple, 42; Microsoft, 43; Intel, 50; HP, 79; and IBM, 107.[93]

The digital revolution does have many weaknesses, however, which will be explained in a later chapter, but it also has many advantages: it increases our knowledge of the world and allows people to globally communicate in real time with others all over the world. We must continue to promote the virtues of the digital revolution and allow everyone to benefit from it. It is amazing to see in our current generations not just millions but billions of people moving from poverty to the world's middle class to now enjoying the benefits of the digital revolution. Many parents are in awe of their children and can't believe the opportunities that they now have in life, which in part has been because of the digital revolution.

In the 21st century, the Republic Earth Organisation is committed to ensuring everyone has access to the digital revolution. We want to ensure that all people can not only access technology anywhere in the world, but also that people living in the global society can access technology affordably.

One area where the digital revolution could make major inroads is with Intelligent Assisting Machines to help people in their homes via new devices such as Amazon's Alexa. Amazon's Alexa allows people to not only obtain news updates, check the weather, check traffic, listen to music, find out general information, make a restaurant reservation etc but in the future it will be able to turn off and on appliances like your air conditioner if the home is fully integrated digitally. We are moving into a world where your home, your car and your tv is all connected digitally to make life easier for people. This is the World of Tomorrow.

This is a small snapshot of the future but the Republic Earth Organisation believes global governance will be needed to protect people from their own personal data being hacked so their home or car is not threatened by a cyber-attack. We want the new Intelligent Assisting Machines to make life easier for people and not cause more problems.[94]

In Australia, under the Rudd and Gillard Labor governments, a forward-thinking new communications network was launched called the National Broadband Network. It was meant to provide fast and reliable broadband to each home and business. After the defeat of the Rudd and Gillard Labor Government in 2013, the Abbott, Turnbull and Morrison coalition governments have turned a once-great idea into a debacle. Instead of creating a fast and reliable service for all Australians, the Abbott, Turnbull and Morrison governments created a two-tier broadband network with a basic service provided to all homes and a requirement to pay more if you wished to obtain a really fast service that was first envisaged under Labor.

This century, it is a requirement that if you live in the middle class in the world you need fast and reliable broadband. Instead of following the lead of other countries like South Korea or Israel that have world-class broadband networks, Australia has short-changed ourselves unnecessarily, which will somewhat undermine our future economic growth in the short term.

The Republic Earth Organisation wants to ensure that all people who live in 600 cities around the world have access to fast and reliable broadband. Australia should take the lead in not only fixing its own broadband problems but assist other nations with gaining access to world-class broadband too. People will increasingly travel more and more, and thus fast and reliable broadband is a requirement for all around the world. The Republic Earth Organisation wants everyone in the global society to enjoy the benefits of the digital revolution in the 21st century.

CHAPTER 12: GENDER EQUALITY and WAVE OF TRANSPARENCY

We have achieved progress towards gender equality and women's empowerment, and we need to continue this work in order to meet the United Nations Millennium Goals, such as ending all forms of discrimination against women and girls everywhere. The Republic Earth Organisation is committed to gender equality and welcomes political developments in countries like Canada, where President Justin Trudeau's 29th Canadian Ministry has 15 men and 15 women, achieving gender equality.[95] In contrast, the SCO, led by China and Russia, is lacking a full commitment to gender equality. For example, the 55th Russian Cabinet has only four women out of 32 people, and within the 19th Politburo of the Communist Party of China, there is only one woman out of 25 people.[96] It is true that the Chinese National Congress has around 24 per cent women and the Russian Federal Assembly has around 16 per cent women; however, when women lack positions in the Russian Cabinet and in the Chinese Politburo, there is a lack of a commitment to gender equality within the SCO.[97]

Gender equality is leading to a more exciting and fairer global society, and we need all nations to be committed to achieving it. Both President Jinping and President Putin would prefer to rule for life than promote gender equality. There appears no appetite in the short or long term in both China and Russia to see a woman become president. In Australia, we are committed to gender equality, and within the Australian Labor Party we will ensure gender equality is achieved in the ministry of a future Labor Government.

Gender equality does not just relate to positions of political power, it is also a commitment to gender equality in all forms of society. For example, the UN Women and the Sustainable Development Goals' targets are to:

- 'end all forms of discrimination against all women and girls everywhere

- eliminate all forms of violence against all women and girls in the public and private spheres, including trafficking and sexual and other types of exploitation

- eliminate all harmful practices, such as child, early and forced marriage and female genital mutilation

- recognize and value unpaid care and domestic work through the provision of public services, infrastructure and social protection policies and the promotion of shared responsibility within the household and the family as nationally appropriate

- ensure women's full and effective participation and equal opportunities for leadership at all levels of decision-making in political, economic and public life

- ensure universal access to sexual and reproductive health and reproductive rights as agreed in accordance with the Programme of Action of the International Conference on Population and Development and the Beijing Platform for Action and the outcome documents of their review conferences

- undertake reforms to give women equal rights to economic resources, as well as access to ownership and control over land and other forms of property, financial services, inheritance and natural resources, in accordance with national laws

- enhance the use of enabling technology, in particular information and communications technology, to promote the empowerment of women

- adopt and strengthen sound policies and enforceable legislation for the promotion of gender equality and the empowerment of all women and girls at all levels'.[98]

Gender equality is not only a fundamental human right, but a necessary foundation for a peaceful, prosperous and sustainable world. Unfortunately, at the current time, one in three women and girls between the ages of 15 and 49 have reported experiencing physical or sexual violence by an intimate partner within a 12-month period, and 49 countries currently have no laws protecting women from domestic violence.[99] Progress is occurring regarding harmful practices such as child marriage and FGM (female genital mutilation), which has declined by 30 per cent in the past decade, but there is still much work to be done to completely eliminate such practices.[100]

Providing women and girls with equal access to education, healthcare, decent work, and representation in political and economic decision-making processes will fuel sustainable economies and benefit societies and humanity at large. Implementing new legal frameworks regarding female equality in the workplace and the eradication of harmful practices targeted at women is crucial to ending the gender-based discrimination prevalent in many countries around the world.

One of the success stories of the gender equality campaign is that we have witnessed a wave of transparency occur showcasing facts about women's pay or women in politics, which has highlighted the injustice that still occurs every day. This wave of transparency has also highlighted shocking facts about the treatment of women. According to the 2018 report on the killing of women and girls released by the UN Office on Drugs and Crime, about 87,000 were killed worldwide in 2017, 58 per cent of them by an intimate partner or relative.[101] Many of these deaths could have been prevented and shows that more work is needed to better protect women and improve the behaviour of men, especially when in an intimate relationship. The goal is to do all we can in the coming years ahead to achieve gender equality as we build the global society.

Wave of Transparency

As mentioned above, we are experiencing an increase in transparency where long-term practices, including the lack of gender equality, are being exposed. Our society is shamed and then work is carried out to address the issue in question. In Australia over recent years, we have had two major Royal Commissions, which have added to this wave of transparency. The Royal Commission into Institutional Responses to Child Sex Abuse exposed endless acts of sexual abuse over decades towards children, while the Royal Commission into Misconduct in the Banking, Superannuation and Financial Services Industry exposed endless acts of financial misconduct, such as charging dead people bank fees. In both cases, these acts were not isolated to Australia but had a global footprint.

The wave of transparency has unveiled acts of misconduct and corruption on a global scale, to the great benefit of citizens around the world. Not only have widespread acts of domestic violence been exposed, but also the widespread acts of citizens, especially elites not paying taxes. The wave of transparency is also moving into the digital revolution and showcasing how little digital companies are regulated and how much power and data they have over people. We must allow the wave of transparency to continue, even though some of the facts that are exposed will be confronting for people to comprehend. Humanity is not perfect but we must expose acts that go against the common good.

The Republic Earth Organisation is committed to creating new enquiries into acts of misconduct, so that the wave of transparency can make our growing global society a better place to live for future generations of humanity.

CHAPTER 13: MEDICAL BREAKTHROUGHS

Recent medical breakthroughs are allowing people to live longer and have better health outcomes than ever before. However, over recent years there have been major disease outbreaks, too, such as the Ebola and Sika viruses, which have killed thousands of people. Thankfully, the trend is that medical breakthroughs are leading to better health outcomes for people all around the world. For example, the world average life expectancy in 1950 was 48 years old, whereas in 2014 it was 71.5 years old.[102]

In terms of the Millennium Development Goals for health, we have made great progress over the last 18 years. For example, 'globally, the number of deaths of children under 5 years of age fell from 12.7 million in 1990 to 6.3 million in 2013. In developing countries, the percentage of underweight children under 5 years old dropped from 28 per cent in 1990 to 17 per cent in 2013. Globally, new HIV infections declined by 38 per cent between 2001 and 2013. Existing cases of tuberculosis are declining, along with deaths among HIV-negative tuberculosis cases. In 2010, the world met the UN Millennium Development Goals target on access to safe drinking water but more has to be done to achieve the sanitation target'.[103]

The Republic Earth Organisation wants to work with the World Health Organization to ensure we continue to improve health outcomes in all areas all around the world. The SCO wants to improve health outcomes, too, but is focused more on improving health outcomes in China rather than all around the world. We need nations to work closely together on major areas of research to cure major diseases and causes of death. For example, one of the great success stories is where 25 research facilities in 19 countries are working together on the Human Proteome Project to identify all of the proteins in the human body, which could have massive ramifications in potentially curing cancers and major diseases.[104] We want more of these projects to be established so that scientists around the world can collaborate on major areas of health research.

According to Meghan Rabbitt, 'This past year has proven to be an equally exciting time for innovative research. Here are some of the most striking medical breakthroughs of 2018 that have potential to change your life: 1) Medical drones...2) Engineered bacteria...3) Medical contact lenses...4) Needle-free injections...5) Sensors that you swallow...6) Medical marijuana...7) New ways to monitor your blood pressure, blood sugar, and body fat and mass index. 8) A system to prevent hair loss from chemotherapy. 9) Comfier mammograms. 10) Smart-imaging computers for cancer prediction.'[105]

One area where medical breakthroughs are occurring is through precision medicine. According to Anthony White (author's brother and Vice President of Business Development at Planet Innovation), 'scientific advances, particularly in genome sequencing, are allowing clinicians to analyse a person's genetic makeup and tailor treatments to suit their needs. One of the areas where precision medicine is making a difference in health care is cancer diagnosis and treatment. Cancer is caused by the uncontrolled, abnormal growth of cells. This growth is driven by mutations—changes in DNA that specially affect genes. For many patients, early and accurate diagnosis is the key for optimal treatment. Indeed, new treatment strategies, such as immunotherapies, require precise classification of the particular molecular subtypes ... Precision medicine has the potential to offer targeted and more effective treatment for diseases such as cancer.'[106]

In recent years we have witnessed many medical advances that need to be congratulated, such as anti-smoking campaigns, which have reduced public smoking, while heart disease has dropped by 40 per cent with a plant based diet, stem cell research has advanced, targeted therapies for cancer have expanded with new drugs, combination drug therapy now extends HIV survival, minimally invasive and robotic techniques are revolutionising surgery, and scientists can peer into the mind with functional MRI.[107]

In the future the Republic Earth Organisation believes that global governance will be needed through the World Health Organization to better protect people's health. For example, according to Yuval Harari, 'if the World Health Organization identifies a new disease, or if a laboratory produces a new medicine, it can't immediately update all the human doctors in the world. Yet even if you had billions of AI doctors in the world—each monitoring the health of a single human being—you could still update all of them within a split second, and they could all communicate to one another their assessments of the new disease or medicine.'[108] The benefits for human society are likely to be immense. The Republic Earth Organisation believes this form of global governance could revolutionise healthcare around the world.

Each year we witness more medical breakthroughs, and we must do all we can to continue to improve health outcomes so the global society can succeed. Nations like Australia, along with other countries, are leading the way in achieving these breakthroughs.

The Republic Earth Organisation wants nations to work more closely together so that all people around the world can enjoy the benefits of medical breakthroughs and have better health outcomes.

CHAPTER 14: GLOBAL GOVERNANCE STRUCTURES

There is a growing need to build new global governance structures, so that the global society can prosper. At present the United Nations, the UN Security Council and the UN's 15 specialised agencies currently play a role in providing a sense of global governance.[109]

There are many other entities, such as the World Trade Organization and the UN Funds and Programmes, such as the Office of the United Nations High Commissioner for Refugees, United Nations Children's Fund, United Nations Development Program, United Nations Environment Programme and the World Food Programme, which are important international entities. However, whereas nation states in the 20th century created entities or departments, such as a Department of Health or Department of Education, in the 21st century we need to have a more global outlook and develop global governance structures instead.[110]

Democratic nations need to unite to form a global organisation, such as a Republic Earth Organisation, to not only help build and develop the global society, but also to address the key global challenges facing humanity today. The Republic Earth Organisation would work with democratic member nations to develop the new World of Order and address the growing World of Disorder. Within the Republic Earth Organisation, new agencies may need to be created to separately address the seven key global challenges currently facing humanity, discussed shortly.

In addition to creating the Republic Earth Organisation, we need to review our international organisations to see which ones are working well and which ones need to be reformed. For example, we currently have a number of economic international organisations including the World Economic Forum, International Monetary Fund and the World Bank, but when capitalism is the global economic system, and the global economy is so interconnected, we need to question whether international economic organisations that were created in the 20th century are still relevant and useful now. In 2019, democratic nations such as Australia should work with other democratic nations to review our international organisations to ensure they are working to help build a global society.

We also argue that to strengthen global governance structures we should create a number of brand-new international organisations to ensure global society succeeds. Most nation states like Australia have government departments that assist with governing the nation. We now need to have a global outlook and think about which government departments could be developed to create a new set of international organisations.

In addition to creating the Republic Earth Organisation, we argue that we need to create 10 new democratic international organisations or entities:

1. Global Planetary Environmental and Renewable Energy Organisation

2. Global Economic and Trade Organisation

3. Global Defence Organisation

4. Global Migration Organisation

5. Global Democracy Organisation

6. Global Education Organisation

7. Global Infrastructure Organisation

8. Global Republic Earth Music Festival

9. Global Communications Network

10. Global Space Agency

Global Planetary Environmental and Renewable Energy Organisation

The Republic Earth Organisation believes that the most important challenge facing humanity in the 21st century is the threat posed by climate change, and thus it is vital to counter this great challenge by establishing a Global Planetary Environmental and Renewable Energy Organisation. On 12 December 2015, at the UN Climate Change Conference, the participating 196 countries agreed, by consensus, to the final global pact, the Paris Agreement, to reduce emissions as part of the method for reducing greenhouse gas.[111] In the 12-page document, the members agreed to reduce their carbon output 'as soon as possible' and to do their best to keep global warming 'to well below 2 degrees C'. In the course of the debates, island states of the Pacific, the Seychelles, but also the Philippines—their very existence threatened by sea level rise—had strongly voted for setting a goal of 1.5 C instead of only 2 C.[112]

It was extremely pleasing that 196 nations united to take action to address climate change, but we also need a united approach to transitioning from an industrial fossil fuel economy to a renewable energy economy and a life-sustaining society. Since the beginning of the industrial revolution nearly two hundred years ago, we have burned immense quantities of coal and gas into the atmosphere and it has now topped four hundred parts per million. According to Bill McKibben, 'the extra heat that we trap near the planet every day is equivalent to the heat from four hundred thousand bombs the size of the one that was dropped on Hiroshima. As a result, in the past thirty years we've seen all twenty of the hottest years ever recorded. The melting of ice caps and glaciers and the rising levels of our oceans and seas, initially predicted for the end of the century, have occurred decades early'.[113]

Due to climate change, we have already managed to kill off 60 per cent of the world's wildlife since 1970 by destroying their habitats, and now higher temperatures are taking their toll.[114] The planet is under unprecedented pressure. Too many forests are being cut down. Too many fish are being pulled out of the seas. Too many species have gone extinct. For the first time in human history, we have pushed the planet too far.

According to a WWF Report from 2018, 'exploding human consumption is the driving force behind unprecedented planetary change we are witnessing, through the increased demand for energy, land and water … While climate change is a growing threat, the main drivers of biodiversity decline continue to be the overexploitation of species, agriculture and land conversion. Indeed, a recent assessment found that only a quarter of land on Earth is substantively free of the impacts of human activities. This is projected to decline to just one-tenth by 2050'.[115] Hence, there cannot be a healthy, happy and prosperous future for people on a planet with a destabilised climate, depleted oceans and rivers, degraded land and empty forests, all stripped of biodiversity; the web of life that sustains us all.

In light of the threat posed by climate change to humanity and the world's wildlife, we need to establish a Global Planetary Environmental and Renewable Energy Organisation. The primary goal will be to quickly build a renewable energy economy and stand up to the fossil fuel industry. In many ways we need to go to war and get the entire world off of fossil fuels by hopefully 2050, and to build a renewable energy economy as quickly as possible. We are on a path to self-destruction if we don't act.

Solar panels and wind turbines are now among the least expensive ways to produce energy. Storage batteries are cheaper and more efficient than ever. We could move quickly if we choose to, but we'd need to opt for solidarity and coordination on a global scale. The concern is that in 2018 leaders in the US, Russia, Saudi Arabia and now Brazil were unwilling to act to address climate change. Despite China wishing to take some action, the SCO and its member nations are addicted to the fossil fuel economy. It has been democratic nations, especially in Scandinavian nations in Europe, that have so far led the way in taking action to address climate change and building a renewable energy economy in their nations. According to Marco Lambertini, Director General of WWF International, 'In the next years, we need to urgently transition to a net carbon-neutral society and halt and reverse nature loss—through green finance and shifting to clean energy and environmentally friendly food production. In addition, we must preserve and restore enough land and ocean in a natural state to sustain all life.'[116]

A country like Australia is perfectly placed to lead efforts to create a Global Planetary Environmental and Renewable Energy Organisation. We have an abundance of renewable energy sources, and some scientists have predicted that if Australia wanted to, we could produce enough renewable energy to power the entire planet. Imagine that. Australia, one of the great fossil fuel, industrial-based economies in the world, has the potential to not only create a 100 per cent renewable energy national economy but also 100 per cent renewable energy global economy.

Australia will never be asked to produce all of the world's energy needs, but we can play a role in assisting many nations with the transition to a renewable energy economy by providing them with forms of renewable energy. One might ask, how can you transfer renewable energy reliably between nations? But with developments in battery storage, it is now easier for a battery to fit into a shipping container, or for intercontinental energy cables to be created under oceans to power other nations. Despite what Australia could possibly do in the future, we must help to unite democratic nations behind a Global Planetary Environmental and Renewable Energy Organisation that better protects Mother Earth.

Not only do we need to create a renewable energy economy but we need to create a life-sustaining society. The world needs a new narrative of Republic Earth—a positive story about new opportunities for humanity to thrive on our beautiful planet by using ingenuity, core values and humanism to become wise stewards of nature and the entire planet. We need to transition away from an industrial growth society to a care and life-sustaining society. If we wait 30 more years, it will be too late. The life-sustaining society is about protecting our biodiversity but also ensuring that potentially half the Earth becomes sustainable and free from human impacts of daily life.

According to Edward Wilson, 'Only by committing half of the planet's surface to nature can we hope to save the immensity of life-forms that compose it ... Unless humanity learns a great deal more about global biodiversity and moves quickly to protect it, we will soon lose most of the species composing life on Earth ... The biosphere does not belong to us; we belong to it. The organisms that surround us in such beautiful profusion are the product of 3.8 billion years of evolution by natural selection ... We are now able to protect the rest of life, but instead we remain recklessly prone to destroy and replace a large part of it.'[117]

Hence, if we create a democratic Global Planetary Environmental and Renewable Energy Organisation that aims to not only create a 100 per cent renewable energy economy but also create a life-sustaining society that protects the world's biodiversity and ensures half the world is protected from the impacts of human life, we can hope to protect Mother Earth.

Global Economic and Trade Organisation

The Republic Earth Organisation is increasingly worried that because democratic nations are beholden to 20th century international economic organisations, the SCO and its member nations have found an opening to exploit so as to expand their economic power at the expense of democratic nations. All nations, including China and Russia, now understand that capitalism rules the international economy and has lifted people out of poverty and turned developing nations into developed nations. Over recent years the SCO, led by China, has sought to undermine the WTO and create an Asian Development Bank in direct competition to the World Bank.[118] We believe we need to counter this economic threat posed by the SCO by establishing a new democratic Global Economic and Trade Organisation.

After World War II, the US helped build a global economic order governed by mutually accepted rules and overseen by multilateral institutions. The idea was to create a better world with countries seeking to cooperate with one another to promote prosperity and peace. Free trade and the rule of law were mainstays of the system, helping to prevent most economic disputes from escalating into larger conflicts. The institutions established included the International Monetary Fund, the UN, the World Bank, the World Trade Organization and NATO. The effect was that we saw more people enter the middle class around the world and capitalism beat communism as the best economic model to advance humanity.

In the 21st century, as capitalism with Chinese characteristics helped lift over 800 million people out of poverty in China into the world's middle class, the Chinese Government decided to not play fairly economically so as to gain an economic advantage.[119] China's rise has been one of the most dominant forces in the global economy. It entered the World Trade Organization in 2001 (the same year the SCO was created) and undertook many reforms, cutting tariffs and other trade barriers.[120] But it still has not completely transformed into a market-oriented economy as its trading partners expected. According to the Australian Foreign Investment Review Board, in many ways there are no private companies in China and they will do what they are told by the Chinese Government.[121]

Many big Chinese companies have close ties with their government, and certain practices have skewed the playing fields on trade. For instance, China unfairly demands that US intellectual property be handed over in certain cases as the price of doing business there.[122] These practices discriminate against Americans but also many other democratic nations, including Australia. To counter these actions by China, the US Trump Administration, starting in March 2018, imposed tariffs on China to change its behaviour. So far, China has only responded by retaliating with tariffs on US goods.[123]

There are ongoing efforts by the EU, the US and Japan to negotiate new rules that would potentially be embedded within the WTO, but these talks are only in the early stages. In contrast, China is forging ahead with the creation of the Regional Comprehensive Economic Partnership with 16 Asian nations to counter the Trans-Pacific Partnership. We argue that the Republic Earth Organisation should encourage democratic nations, led by the US, EU nations, Japan and Australia, to counter the economic challenges being posed by the SCO led by China and Russia that wish to change the global economic rules in their favour.

The worry is the US Trump Administration rejection of globalisation and putting America first, is allowing China an opening to become the global economic superpower of the 21st century and to build an autocratic and repressive economic world order. In the next decade, democratic nations need to unite to protect the current democratic rules-based economic order, and thus to do so we should consider establishing a new democratic Global Economic and Trade Organisation. The global market still has great potential for every nation and thus we must allow it to work for all nations and not just a few like China and Russia in the future.

We live in a global economy and if a nation has an economic downturn, we are all affected. Only the creation of a democratic Global Economic and Trade Organisation will protect us from any future global economic meltdown. A Global Economic and Trade Organisation will also help address the growing threat of inequality and help to build a stronger and more robust global middle class, to the benefit of all citizens around the world.

The organisation should also address the concerns of the harm caused by the digital revolution and rein in the unaccountable power of it. The digital revolution is helping to create the World of Order but it is also causing harm in the World of Disorder, and thus we need to establish a democratic Global Economic and Trade Organisation to counter these adverse effects. In particular, the Republic Earth Organisation believes we need to monitor Chinese digital companies that have close connections to the Chinese Government, and thus the autocratic SCO.

Private Internet/Digital Companies by Market Value: 29 May 2018

US (Democratic)	China (Autocratic)
1 Apple	6 Alibaba
2 Amazon	7 Tencent
3 Microsoft	9 Ant Financial
4 Google	13 Baidu
5 Facebook	14 Xiaomi
6 Netflix	16 Didi Chuxing
10 eBay + Paypal	17 JD.com
11 Booking Holdings	19 Meituan-Dianping
12 Salesforce.com	20 Toutiao

15 Uber	
18 Airbnb	
124	

We need to ensure that we allow the digital revolution to work for all global citizens. We do not want Chinese digital companies to unfairly monitor citizens in a repressive manner when people already accept democratic values around the world. China and President Jinping have big plans. According to Graham Allison, 'By 2025, China means to be the dominant power in the major market in 10 leading technologies, including driverless cars, robots, artificial intelligence, quantum computing. By 2035, China means to be the innovation leader across all the advanced technologies. And by 2049, which is the 100th anniversary of the founding of the People's Republic, China means to be unambiguously number one, including, [says] Xi Jinping, an army that he calls "Fight and Win". So these are audacious goals, but as you can see, China is already well on its way to these objectives. And we should remember how fast our world is changing. Thirty years ago, the World Wide Web had not yet even been invented.'[125]

The world will rapidly change in the next 30 years, but the digital revolution has to be regulated to work for all citizens. We need to create a Global Economic and Trade Organisation to ensure the digital revolution works for the benefit of all of humanity and does not continue to cause harm around the world.

The Global Economic and Trade Organisation should also establish a Global Bank that aims to better assist citizens everywhere. At present, the World Bank is not used by citizens for banking services. Australia could lead the way in establishing a new Global Bank, backed up by reserves from member nations of the Republic Earth Organisation, so that people around the world can use this banking services. Citizens could use the services of a private bank or could use the services of a new public Global Bank. Australia has four major banks and a strong banking system, yet a recent Royal Commission into Australia's banking system has showcased failures. The building of a public Global Bank would not only be welcomed by Australians but by citizens around the world.[126]

Global Defence Organisation

The Republic Earth Organisation would like to see democratic nations unite to create a brand-new Global Defence Organisation, or a Global Defence Alliance. After World War II, the United Nations was established to create a more united world; however, with new global security threats, a rise in authoritarianism, and the emergence of the SCO, the world seems to be becoming less united.

At present, democratic nations have a range of defence alliances; however, the preeminent democratic defence organisation is NATO, which consists of 29 member states from North America and Europe, including: Albania, Belgium, Bulgaria, Canada, Croatia, Czech Republic, Denmark, Estonia, France, Germany, Greece, Hungary, Iceland, Italy, Latvia, Lithuania, Luxembourg, Montenegro, the Netherlands, Norway, Poland, Portugal, Romania, Slovakia, Spain, Turkey, United Kingdom and the United States.[127] While countries like Australia and New Zealand have an ANZUS alliance with the United States.

The Republic Earth Organisation believes that NATO should be reformed to become the democratic Global Defence Organisation, or we should simply create a brand-new democratic Global Defence Organisation to counter the rise in authoritarianism and the emergence of the autocratic SCO. This would mean NATO member nations would be joined by democratic countries such as Australia, New Zealand, Japan, Indonesia, South Korea, India, etc. The new democratic Global Defence Organisation should have a key policy like NATO's Article Five, which states that if an armed attack occurs against one of the member states, it should be considered an attack against all members, and other members shall assist the attacked member, with armed forces if necessary.[128]

The goal of the Global Defence Organisation should be to encourage all nations to become democratic and to become members of this new global democratic defence alliance by the end of the 21st century. This may seem like a utopian goal, but if most nations are part of this organisation then we have a higher chance of achieving world peace. Since World War II, we have lost our way in creating a more united and peaceful world, and thus encouraging more nations to join a democratic global organisation is vital to achieve this goal.

The Republic Earth Organisation also believes that the creation of a Global Defence Organisation should be tasked with addressing three of the concerns in the World of Disorder; that is, the increase in terrorism and cyberterrorism, the increase in the threat posed by nuclear weapons, and the increase in foreign influence and autocratic nations threatening democratic nations. The Global Defence Organisation should be tasked with working on policies to counter each of these threats, so that we create a more united and peaceful world.

Global Migration Organisation

The Republic Earth Organisation believes we need to create a Global Migration Organisation to counter one of the key challenges in the World of Disorder posed by the rapid increase in the numbers of displaced people and refugees, which now totals over 68 million.[129] This challenge only seems to be increasing due to the threats of climate change and conflict or terrorism within nations. It is pleasing that the United Nations invited member nations to an Intergovernmental Conference to Adopt the Global Compact for Safe, Orderly and Regular Migration held in Marrakech, Morocco, on 10-11 December 2018. This Global Compact set out a common understanding, shared responsibilities and unity of purpose regarding migration.

According to the Global Compact, it offered 'a 360-degree vision of international migration and recognises that a comprehensive approach is needed to optimise the overall benefits of migration, while addressing risks and challenges for individuals and communities in countries of origin, transit and destination. No country can address the challenges and opportunities of this global phenomenon on its own. With a comprehensive approach, it aims to facilitate safe, orderly and regular migration, while reducing the incidence and negative impact of irregular migration through International cooperation and a combination of measures put forward in this Global Compact ... The Global Compact for Migration:

- aims to mitigate the adverse drivers and structure factors that hinder people from building and maintaining sustainable livelihoods in their country of origin;

- intends to reduce the risks and vulnerabilities migrants face at different stages of migration by respecting, protecting and fulfilling their human rights and providing them with care and assistance;

- seeks to address legitimate concerns of communities, while recognising that societies are undergoing demographic, economic, social and environmental changes at different scales that may have implications for and result from migration;

- strives to create conducive conditions that enable all migrants to enrich our societies through their human, economic and social capacities, and thus facilitate their contributions to sustainable development at the local, national, regional and global levels.'[130]

The Republic Earth Organisation believes that the creation of a Global Migration Organisation will help to achieve the Global Compact objectives for safe, orderly and regular migration, which are:

1. 'Collect and utilize accurate and disaggregated data as a basis for evidence-based policies

2. Minimize the adverse drivers and structural factors that compel people to leave their country of origin

3. Provide adequate and timely information at all stages of migration

4. Ensure that all migrants have proof of legal identity and adequate documentation

5. Enhance availability and flexibility of pathways for regular migration

6. Facilitate fair and ethical recruitment and safeguard conditions that ensure decent work

7. Address and reduce vulnerabilities in migration

8. Save lives and establish coordinated international efforts on missing migrants

9. Strengthen the transnational response to smuggling of migrants

10. Prevent, combat and eradicate trafficking in persons in the context of international migration

11. Manage borders in an integrated, secure and coordinated manner

12. Strengthen certainty and predictability in migration procedures for appropriate screening, assessment and referral

13. Use migration detention only as a measure of last resort and work towards alternatives

14. Enhance consular protection, assistance and cooperation throughout the migration cycle

15. Provide access to basic services for migrants

16. Empower migrants and societies to realize full inclusion and social cohesion

17. Eliminate all forms of discrimination and promote evidence-based public discourse to shape perceptions of migration

18. Invest in skills development and facilitate mutual recognition of skills, qualifications and competences

19. Create conditions for migrants and diasporas to fully contribute to sustainable development in all countries

20. Promote faster, safer and cheaper transfer of remittances and foster financial inclusion of migrants

21. Cooperate in facilitating safe and dignified return, readmission, as well as sustainable reintegration

22. Establish mechanisms for the portability of social security entitlements and earned benefits

23. Strengthen international cooperation and global partnerships for safe, orderly and regular migration.'[131]

In Australia, the Coalition Government has decided to not sign up to the Global Compact, but when we are dealing with a global problem, we need a global solution.[132] If a nation has problems with the Global Compact they should provide alternative ideas rather than rejecting a global solution outright. The worry is that we may have more displaced peoples and refugees in the future, so we desperately need to create a Global Migration Organisation to deal with this threat, especially when there is a lack of leadership on this issue from the SCO.

Global Democracy Organisation

The Republic Earth Organisation aims to create a global democracy, but it is vital that it is created to spread democratic values around the world. In particular, the Global Democracy Organisation should act as an international electoral commission to monitor elections around the world. Nearly every nation has a parliament, but according to the Democracy Index we have a range of nations that are full democracies, flawed democracies, hybrid regimes and authoritarian regimes. The aim of the Global Democracy Organisation would be to assist all nations to become full democracies and to offer assistance of providing expert support during national elections.

The Global Democratic Organisation would offer a service to nations, so that everybody's voice is heard and to counter acts of corruption and autocratic rule. In Australia we have the Australian Electoral Commission that runs our national elections, and while they make mistakes, they are one of the most respected democratic institutions in the world. Therefore, Australia can lead the way in helping to build a Global Democratic Organisation. Another aim would be to have more women in parliament in all nations. Women now comprise the largest share of the US House of Representatives in history at 23 per cent, but still much less than in Australia at 27 per cent, Germany at 31 per cent and France at 39 per cent.[133] In light of the emergence of the SCO, it is vital that a Global Democratic Organisation is created to counter the decline in democracy and rise in authoritarianism.

Global Infrastructure Organisation

The Republic Earth Organisation believes that democratic nations need to urgently create a Global Infrastructure Organisation to counter the threat posed by the SCO with its Belt and Road Initiative (BRI), which currently involves 86 countries.[134] The BRI is a development strategy by the SCO and the Chinese Government to invest in infrastructure development and investment in countries around the world. China, through the BRI, has used a form of sharp power to gain greater influence and power in other nations. Even in Australia, the state of Victoria signed the BRI in October 2018, showcasing that even democratic countries are susceptible to the growing power and influence of China and the SCO.[135]

We argue that democratic nations need to counter this threat and create a Global Infrastructure Organisation instead to assist nations with new infrastructure projects and investments. We cannot sit back and cede power to autocratic nations like China and Russia, so that they can control global affairs in the 21st century. A nation like Australia cannot only be involved in infrastructure projects and investment in Pacific countries, and the might of China will easily beat Australia with sharp power. However, if all democratic nations unite to create a Global Infrastructure Organisation, then we can successfully counter the threat posed by the BRI and the SCO.

Post-World War II, the United States, through the Marshall Plan, began to appreciate how devastated Europe was and how aggressive Soviet communism was, and thus Americans eventually decided to tax themselves a per cent and a half of GDP every year for four years and send that money to Europe to help reconstruct these countries, including Germany and Italy, whose troops had just been killing Americans.[136] As a result, Europe was able to be rebuilt after the devastation caused by the war. Through the Republic Earth Organisation, we need to create a new global Marshall Plan to not only help citizens join the world's middle class but also to counter the threat posed by the autocratic Belt and Road Initiative. This new organisation would be perfectly placed to get all member nations, through either government programs or taxes, to play a role in investing in all nations and all citizens, provided nations want that assistance.

Global Education Organisation

The Republic Earth Organisation wishes to develop policies to invest heavily in education as we enter the age of human capital. We want to make sure that everyone in the global middle class can obtain a first-class education in the 21st century. But to help coordinate higher education at a global level, we need to create a Global Education Organisation. We believe that most nations will wish to govern their childcare, preschool, primary school and high school education systems. However, as we continue to develop a global society, it will be increasingly more important to offer a globalised form of higher education where many degrees have a global standard, allowing people to apply for jobs with that qualification in many nations. One of the key emerging problems is that people may complete a degree in one country only to then have to move to another country and complete a new but similar degree to meet the necessary national requirements of that country. The creation of a Global Education Organisation will encourage member nations to unite to agree on a global standard for many degrees.

It is exciting that the developing world is becoming developed, and we hope that everyone in the future will be able to get a wonderful education no matter where they live. In terms of Australia, we have had an education advantage over many nations for the last 200 years; however,

70

that is about to change as, increasingly, more people enter the world's middle class and gain a full education. By 2050 at the latest, all people will be connected to the digital revolution, and if all 9.7 billion people are trying to be original then it will be an exciting time in the age of human capital![137] Imagine a world where 9.7 billion people are constantly adding and exchanging new ideas on a daily basis.

Australia should play a role in exporting our high-quality education services to the rest of the world. Many developing nations are craving these services and Australia can play a soft power role by increasingly trying to educate people everywhere. At the same time as exporting education services around the world, we should modernise our own childcare, schools and higher education services to make them the best in the world.

One of the leading educational thinkers at present is Sir Ken Robinson, who has become famous through his world-renowned TED Talks. Robinson has suggested that to engage and succeed, education has to develop on three fronts: 'First, that it should foster diversity by offering a broad curriculum and encourage individualism of the learning process. Second, it should foster curiosity through creative teaching, which depends on high quality teacher training and development. Finally, it should focus on awakening creativity through alternative didactic processes that put less emphasis on standardised testing, thereby giving responsibility for defining the course of education to individual schools and teachers.'[138] Robinson believes that much of the present education system in the United States or Australia fosters conformity, compliance and standardisation rather than creative approaches to learning. We need to modernise our education systems in democratic nations so as to value students being creative and original. We should not simply provide students with an ATAR score that not only defines their high school experience but sets out what they can or cannot do at a higher educational level.

This book embodies this spirit of creativity and originality. As someone who is passionate about politics, we cannot simply follow the current state of Australian politics. It is vital to assess the state of Australian politics and come up with new ideas, such as the idea of a Republic

Earth, which is a new political theory that aims to not only establish a global democracy but also assist with creating global governance to make sure that all citizens succeed in the 21st century. In the age of human capital, happiness lies in the joy of achievement and the thrill of creative effort, so let's encourage more people to be original and creative.

The Republic Earth Organisation understands that each country has a unique education system but wants to help work out what works best in other countries. If Australia can improve its childcare system by adopting some of Sweden's policies, then other countries can do the same in different parts of their education systems. The Republic Earth Organisation is concerned that the SCO is not committed to ensuring that everyone in the world has a first-class education and that their freedom of thought is likely to be curtailed. Unfortunately, it is a regular process in China for students to be arrested if they speak out for the need of democracy in China. We believe that such acts by China and Russia; for example, of locking up students as dissidents for promoting democracy, is unacceptable and only curtails their freedoms. Imagine in the future that the SCO sets the global rules for education based on these rules. Millions of students around the world would be locked up as dissidents for promoting democracy.

The Republic Earth Organisation believes that in creating a Global Education Organisation we are not only helping to create a global standard for degrees in higher education, but also allowing nations to develop better education systems and share good ideas, as well as protect democratic free speech for students around the world.

Global Republic Earth Music Festival

The Republic Earth Organisation believes that the power of music can help create a global democracy and build a global society in the 21st century. In Australia, we hold one of the great democratic music festivals—the Triple J's Hottest 100—where Australians vote for their favourite 10 songs for the year, and the votes are then tallied up to form the Hottest 100 songs that are played each year on Triple J Radio. The goal of the Republic Earth Organisation is to take this idea that has become increasingly popular and make it global, so that people all around the world can vote for their favourite songs via a brand-new multicultural Republic Earth Music Festival in the lead up to New Year's Eve each year.

The Republic Earth Organisation believes that Melbourne in Australia should become the home of this festival. It is important to point out that more than a quarter of Melbourne's population were born over-seas, with the people speaking more than 260 languages and dialects, coming from over 200 different countries, and sharing 135 different faiths.[139] To celebrate Melbourne being one of the most multicultural cities, we believe the Melbourne Cricket Ground (MCG) should host the Republic Earth Music Festival on New Year's Eve each year.

Between 26th December and 31st December, people all around the world would be invited to vote online or via social media for their favourite 10 songs from that year to form part of the festival. Each song has to have been popular in the particular calendar year of the festival. The festival will showcase the most popular songs or 'the people's' songs from that particular year from each country in the world. The aim would be to hold the event between 6pm and 10pm local time, with 36 songs being showcased.

Prior to the festival, there would be a parade of singers with national flags to promote where each artist/band has come from. At 10pm Melbourne time, the festival will trigger **three separate global count-downs or parties: first,** a major 24-hour NYE countdown of the 216 most popular songs, as voted by people all around the world; **second,** an additional 24-hour NYE countdown to acknowledge the most popular songs from each of the IOC National Olympic Committee member states plus South Sudan (that totals 206 nations), six of the world's most pop-ular songs via sales and online popularity, and four songs from different indigenous peoples around the world, which makes a total of 216 songs; **third,** a 24-hour party in each country, where music will be performed to celebrate and promote the need for a more united world.

The Republic Earth Music Festival would be a significant global event that has the potential to have a large global television audience, as well as being streamed live online via Facebook, YouTube, Vevo and Twitter. The Republic Earth Organisation believes that most people will want to vote, participate and enjoy the music performed as part of the festival each year. On New Year's Day each year at 10pm in Sydney, the plan is to announce the winner of the most popular song voted by people around the world. Finally, after each festival, a golden record could be created of the music from that festival, and that record should be released into space or form part of a mission to showcase humanity's music to the cosmos. While Eurovision helps to bring Europe together, we believe the Republic Earth Music Festival can play a role in bringing the whole world together for the common good.

Global Communications Network

The Republic Earth Organisation is committed to building a new global communications network. In the 20th century, governments set up their own television and radio networks. In Australia, for example, the government primarily funds the Australian Broadcasting Corporation (ABC) and the Special Broadcasting Service (SBS). Both investments are greatly valued by the Australian people.

However, this century there is the opportunity for the Republic Earth Organisation, led by Australia when English is the world's de facto global language, to create the first government-funded global television and radio network. At present, we see no interest from primarily English-speaking countries, such as Great Britain, Ireland, USA, Canada, South Africa or elsewhere, to create the first governmental global network. China may wish to create a network but it will struggle to do so while English is the de facto global language. Accordingly, in the future under a Labor Government, the Australian Government, with the support of the Republic Earth Organisation, has the unique opportunity to create the first government-funded global television and radio network, which could be called Republic Earth. The Republic Earth Television and Radio Network would work in partnership with all government-controlled media networks in each country. As a result, all the content from Australia's ABC and SBS stations would be linked to the Republic Earth Network. While all the content from the UK's BBC would also be linked to the Republic Earth Network, and so on for each participating country.

We have seen the rise of Netflix and how a private television network has gone global quickly due to the benefits of the digital revolution. However, we have not seen the same transition occur with govern-ment-controlled networks. Global citizens have many fears about the creation of global governmental television networks because they do not want one created and used for government surveillance in a George Orwell *1984* style. Accordingly, the Republic Earth Organisation is wor-ried that if the SCO grows in power and influence, it is likely to create global communications networks with such ends.

For example, in Australia our intelligence agencies have been increas-ingly concerned with China's Huawei in relation to security risks over its data collection.[140] We are concerned that the SCO, through companies like Huawei, is gaining sensitive data about people's lives around the world. This is an infringement of civil liberties and we need to protect our privacy. It is true that many Western corporations are also accessing similar data, but in Western nations we can hold companies to account for privacy breaches.

We should look closely at companies like Huawei and hold them to ac-count for data breaches. The Republic Earth Organisation understands that it is possible for the first time in history to watch live any television channel anywhere around the world provided the television is connect-ed to the internet. If we can work on a project to connect all public television channels in every country to the internet, then when you are holidaying in say Bali, Indonesia, you can turn on your television and as an Australian tourist watch all the ABC channels, or as an English tourist all the BBC channels. There will always be commercial television net-works, but if nations joined together to create a Republic Earth Televi-sion and Radio Network, it would be truly exciting and would assist in bringing the world together for the common good.

Young people increasingly see themselves as global citizens, and there is an opportunity for Australia, with the support of the Republic Earth Organisation, to go beyond just funding national media networks and instead fund a global media network. Australia is arguably the most multicultural country in the world, and it only seems fitting that we are the nation to create this network.

Imagine a world where you return home from work in Melbourne, Australia, and you turn on your television and ask it to go to live Brazilian television, or live Estonian television or live Togo television. This is the world of tomorrow. In light of the digital revolution and the internet, it is now possible to connect to any television channel anywhere in the world. At present we have many government restrictions on what can be shared. For example, there are different Apple stores for each country and different Netflix stores for each country.[141] A Global Republic Earth Media Network would wish to break down those restrictions, geo blocs and media barriers. No longer would you have to wait several months to watch a television show from France. If it is released in France it should be seen as released to the world and thus open to the people of the world to watch it.

To begin with, all governmental networks would need to connect to the Republic Earth Media Network. Afterwards, the goal would be to connect all private channels and it would be up to you to purchase them if you wished to; however, it would become an easier way to access any television channel in the world. In the future there could be a series of global governmental and private television and radio channels, and a series of current national-based governmental and private channels. As global citizens it will be up to you to choose from the new world of possibilities.

The creation of a democratic Global Media Network would also help to counter the information war being launched by the SCO via Chinese State TV and Russia Today. According to the director of the BBC World Service Group, Jamie Angus, 'you will increasingly find Russia Today present in the top 10 channels in American hotels and that is because they pay to be there'. He adds there is a growing issue about where English-speaking people get their international news from and there is a concerted effort from China and Russia, and to a lesser extent Turkey, to own the English-language international news space. He goes on to say, 'I think we are in a global information war.'[142] Hence the need for democratic nations to unite against this threat. At present we have CNN (USA), BBC World News (UK), France 24 (France) and DW News (Germany), but we need to unite to create one major global English-language media network. There is still a place for national broadcasters and news networks, but if we had news coming from all countries and all networks into one network, then that would be amazing. Australia can be at the forefront of creating this new global media network to counter the threat posed by China, Russia and the SCO.

The creation of a Republic Earth Media Network may well help to create a new renaissance, as for the first time people would have access to all television and radio from everywhere. It would open people's minds to other cultures and languages. It may help reduce tensions between countries and bring the world together for the common good. The United Nations should have led the way with creating such a network, but has failed to do so. However, when the US is dealing with the adverse effects of a Donald Trump Presidency, the UK is dealing with Brexit, and China and Russia are trying to turn global rules and norms to their favour, there is a unique opportunity for Australia, as a middle power, to use its strength of being so multicultural to build the global governance in the 21st century. In terms of communications, this means we should be working towards creating the first global democratic governmental media network.

Global Space Agency

The Republic Earth Organisation is also committed to creating a global space agency. In 2017, the Australian Government began the journey of considering the best way to create a national space agency to cash in on a $420 billion aeronautical industry and create thousands of new jobs.[143] It is interesting that it has taken so long for Australia to consider creating a space agency, especially when we have the 13th largest economy in the world.[144] However, Australia should not just consider creating a national space agency but instead work with the Republic Earth Organisation to create a *global* space agency.

As of 2017, 72 different government space agencies exist.[145] Thirteen of those have launch capabilities, while six—the Indian Space Research

Organisation (ISRO), the European Space Agency (ESA), the China National Space Administration (CNSA), the Japan Aerospace Exploration Agency (JAXA), the National Aeronautics and Space Administration (NASA), and the Russian Federal Space Agency (RFSA or Roscosmos)—have full launch capabilities.[146] However, only three space agencies in the world—RFSA, CNSA and NASA—were capable of human space flight in 2017.[147]

In the next 10 years we are going to see a radical transformation in the space industry, and it is vital that Australia is an active participant. For example, Space X's founder Elon Musk has stated that his spaceship, dubbed the BFR, would carry about 100 people, and could be used in the first instance to fly to any city in the world in less than 60 minutes.[148] He painted a picture of people boarding a ship in New York City and heading to Shanghai in just 39 minutes.[149] In Australia, we are starting the process of building a second Sydney International Airport, but what we need to consider is whether building space airports in each major city to cater for our future needs would be more appropriate. We need to be in the process of building the world of the future.

It is argued that the Australian Government should strongly consider creating a space agency but not necessarily a national space agency. Australia should consider creating a global space agency. The EU helped to create the European Space Agency. While countries like Germany and Spain have national space agencies, most work is carried out by the ESA. Accordingly, Australia should work with all nations to create a global space agency.

It is predicted that human beings may have the potential to travel to Mars by 2030; however, it would be a pity if a nation such as Russia, China or the US achieved the goal of humanity walking on Mars on the back of a nationalistic agenda. If humanity was to set foot on Mars, then it is an achievement that the whole of humanity should take pride in. In many ways, the entire history of humanity would have got us to that moment of reaching another planet in our solar system, and thus the achievement must be seen as a triumph for humanity and the citizens of Republic Earth, and not simply an achievement for any one country or any one private company. In addition, the SCO is not planning to create a global space agency, so there is a window of opportunity for a country like Australia to show global leadership by creating one.

The United Nations does have a space agency but it should be working harder to create a formal global space agency, which it has failed to do so.[150] Instead, Australia when it is in the process of creating a national space agency for the first time it can also help to create a global space agency.

It is vital that a form of global governance regulates and monitors the future rapid growth in space exploration. If we allow it to go unchecked, then a business or a nation state could gain space superiority with unintended and unfair consequences. Also, it is better for nations to work together. Each nation and each private company needs to think about the common good and not just their own self-interests.

In the 21st century, Australia is an exciting place to live, work and raise a family, but we need to seize the opportunity of the space revolution and not just create a national space agency but a global space agency that brings the world together for the common good.

A World Parliament

The Republic Earth Organisation believes that it may be possible in the future to create a European Union style Global Parliament but at the very least we should recognise that each parliamentarian representing an electorate in a nation is a member of an imagined Global Parliament or a Republic Earth Parliament, and he or she should be sent a global badge to recognise this fact. According to the Inter-Parliamentary Union, 'almost all the countries in the world have some form of functioning parliamentary institution. There are 46,552 members of parliament in the world. The global average number of parliamentarians per country is 245. China has the largest parliament with 3,000 members in the Chinese National People's Congress. The world's smallest parliament is in Micronesia, with just 14 MPs. The global average number of inhabitants per parliamentarian is 146,000, although in India that number is 1.5 million inhabitants per MP. San Marino has the smallest number at 517. There are 8,716 women parliamentarians globally, which is 19.25 per cent of the total number of MPs. New IPU figures on women MPs supersede these.'[151]

One day this century it would be exciting to invite all members from parliaments from around the world to a special (noting the valid national security risks), once-in-a-lifetime event to meet, such as at the MCG in Melbourne, to recognise the need to bring the world together for the common good. It would be too difficult to have all members around the world participate in a 'World Parliament' on a daily basis (unless a separate European Union style Global Parliament was created), but each member of parliament from around the world should be invited to play an ongoing role in building the World of Order and countering the World of Disorder and the key global challenges facing humanity.

CHAPTER 15: REPUBLIC EARTH—NEW LIBERAL DEMOCRATIC WORLD OF ORDER

We are not only in a battle between the World of Order and the World of Disorder; we are in a battle to maintain our liberal democratic way of life or else witness a new authoritarian world emerge. It is true that the liberal, democratic World of Order has led to 3.2 billion people joining the world's middle class, and unlike under communism, fascism or authoritarianism, we are witnessing people achieve better education outcomes, better job opportunities and better health outcomes.[152] However, this liberal, democratic way of life has come under threat because the industrial growth society has not created a fair and equal society but has led to economic inequality. The industrial growth society has also led to man-made climate change, which is threatening humanity. We need a new story; a story where we transition from an industrial growth society to a life-sustaining society for the benefit of all.

The idea of a Republic Earth—a fresh and positive view of our new emerging global society—could be the new story humanity is looking for. Mother Earth is suffering and is under threat from climate change, but over the coming decades we need to create a grand, global coalition to counter this threat and protect our planet for future generations. Former US President Robert Kennedy famously said that we can keep thinking about the benefits of an industrial growth society and the value of our gross domestic product, but think more about our gross national product that counts air pollution and cigarette advertising, and thus making the case for a larger view of the world.[153] Why do we keep using plastic on a large scale if it is killing our oceans? Why do we promote sugar when we are seeing an increase in deaths from obesity and diabetes? Why do we continue to embrace an industrial growth society when the top two per cent of people own more than half the world's wealth? It is time we told a new story for humanity; a better life-sustaining story for humanity- a Republic Earth.

One of the main threats to a liberal, democratic Republic Earth is authoritarianism and fascism. The SCO wishes to take control of the world but its autocratic and fascist views will greatly harm humanity because democratic freedoms will be suppressed. At a time when we could be about to embark on a great new renaissance in education breakthroughs, artistic breakthroughs, health breakthroughs, economic breakthroughs and technological breakthroughs, we cannot allow an autocratic worldview to stifle humanity's creativity. In the coming decades we could have record levels of people entering the world's middle class, and an explosion of exchanging new ideas globally, instantly and at zero cost. Or we could have people subjected to an autocratic social credit system envisaged by the SCO that wishes to monitor people's behaviour like an Orwellian police state. I expect that this global world is not the world we would like to see created, but for leaders such as President Jinping and President Putin it is their dream and it is within their grasp, as silently we are falling into this world.

One of the biggest threats from the SCO is their wish to have the world's most powerful military and economy at the expense of all others. It is true that the US did politically interfere with many nations during the 20th century, but while having the most powerful military and economy it did everything it could to increase the global middle class and allow countries to grow economically unimpeded. In contrast, China wishes to dominate at the expense of all others, and it will compete hard to maintain global supremacy in the 21st century in military or economic terms. The big problem is that President Jinping has a China First Strategy, while President Putin has a Russia First Strategy. Even President Trump has an America First Strategy. French President Macron does have a slightly different Europe First Strategy. But what is needed is a World First Strategy. We need to move away from simply thinking in the national interest and understand that we have too many global issues to address, and thus the only way forward is to think in the global interest.

Republic Earth is about putting the world first, and Australia could be the first nation in the world to make the case for a World First Strategy. Republic Earth wants all nations and all people to benefit in the 21st century. Too often, China's sharp power strategy in Africa or Asia has meant that it brings in its own workforce to build a project, creating an economic debt in the country in question.[154] While a country may welcome the investment, it is all in China's interest for the project to occur in the first place. In contrast, Republic Earth wishes to help all countries and invest in all people around the world, provided they believe in democracy. Unfortunately, nations will have to make a choice of whether they wish to support a global autocratic worldview put forward by China and the SCO, or whether they will support a global democratic worldview put forward by Australia and the Republic Earth Organisation. Will they support another worldview, or will they remain independent?

The global democratic worldview, a World First Strategy or a Republic Earth Strategy, is the best way forward for humanity in the 21st century.

One may argue that a World First Strategy could undermine a country's national agenda, but it will not. All we are trying to do is to continue to bring the world together for the common good. For example, during the 2018 FIFA World Cup, no one can deny that fans were not patriotically supporting their own country, and every nation's spirit was fantastic. This is what is exciting about bringing nations together; we can showcase the brilliance of each nation. Republic Earth wants to showcase the brilliance of every nation, whereas the SCO wants to showcase just the brilliance of China.

For centuries, major powers have showcased their exceptional natures, but we need to end this. No more exceptionalism. We should be showcasing the brilliance of all nations and the diversity of humanity. The goal in the future is to encourage the US to move away from exceptionalism and embrace the world. If it does, it will mark an important moment in world history and be of great benefit to the world. If US exceptionalism continues in conjunction with Chinese exceptionalism, then conflict becomes more likely. Republic Earth believes in nations putting the planet and the world first, as this is the only way to grow the global society and the new World of Order so as to successfully address the key challenges posed by the World of Disorder, and finally create a more peaceful and united world.

Republic Earth Organisation

The Republic Earth agenda has two basic goals:

1. To celebrate the emergence of the new global society (and develop a World First Strategy), which is being led by young millennials who see themselves not only as citizens of a nation state but also as global citizens. We are now seeing young people increasingly travel overseas, listen to music from around the world and eat global cuisine. We need to celebrate the emergence of the new global society and allow it to grow and prosper.

2. To create a global democracy. According to Gideon Rose, there is a case for a fourth founding of the Liberal Democratic Order or a fourth attempt to create a global democracy.[155] Democratic nations have tried three times to unite the world under a liberal, democratic, global agenda. After World War I, democratic nations created the League of Nations but it failed. After World War II, democratic nations created the United Nations, which still exists and plays a major role in solving global issues, but after 74 years the world has yet to become fully united under a liberal, democratic, global agenda. After the Cold War, the G7 emerged as the preeminent body to lead the democratic agenda, but since 2001 it has been distracted and has lost its focus on uniting the world under a liberal, democratic, global agenda. Accordingly, by creating a Republic Earth Organisation, we can work in partnership with the UN to finally succeed in a fourth attempt to unite the world based on a liberal, democratic, global agenda, which achieves the goal of creating a **global democracy**.

Hopefully, a Republic Earth liberal, democratic world order will become the new, exciting experience that citizens and nations all around the world have been looking for in the 21st century. It has huge potential but needs support. Australia can lead the way in making the case for this democratic world order with a World First Strategy.

PART 2

THE WORLD OF DISORDER BATTLE IN THE 21ST CENTURY

Ω

We are involved in a global battle to address the growing World of Disorder. The Republic Earth Organisation is fully committed to addressing the key global challenges facing the world this century.

We currently need to address seven key global challenges:

1. Increase in climate change threats.

2. Increase in inequality.

3. Increase in terrorism and cyberterrorism.

4. Increase in displaced people and refugees.

5. Increase in economic and social harm caused by the digital revolution, meaning we need to rein in the unaccountable power associated with it.

6. Increase in the threat posed by nuclear weapons.

7. Increase in autocratic regimes threatening democratic nations.

It is true that the world faces many other global challenges, including the inability to end wars in Syria and Yemen, Palestine and Israel, the continued use of chemical weapons, the continued increase in disease outbreaks in the form of the Ebola and Zika viruses, and the human rights agenda losing ground. However, while each of these and many others are global challenges, the priority has to be for democratic nations to unite together to combat the seven key global challenges listed above, because if we can do so then the global society will be able to grow and prosper.

It is vital that a democratic international organisation such as a Republic Earth Organisation is created to coordinate a global response among nations to counter these global challenges. In 1933, when US President Roosevelt came to power, he developed a number of initiatives to counter the Great Depression. Some of these worked and some did not, but he knew that he had no choice but to offer a new deal to the American people. In the end, Roosevelt created a war against the Great Depression and he emerged victorious. In the 21st century, democratic nations need to adhere to the same strategy and create a war against the seven key global challenges facing humanity. Some initiatives will work and some may not, but we must do all we can to counter each challenge so that the World of Disorder does not escalate.

The SCO and its member nations are actually contributing to the World of Disorder so as to gain a competitive edge in the geopolitical battles to control the world. The nations that co-founded the SCO—China and Russia—are using cyberterrorism and a new form of sharp power to undermine and steal power away from democratic nations. Instead of offering a different alternative to the liberal, democratic, capitalist, industrial-growth society that has contributed to man-made climate change and an increase in inequality, the SCO has simply moved away from communism and embraced the capitalist, industrial-growth society, adding to an increase in climate change threats and an increase in inequality.

It is interesting that the former leading communist nations of the 20th century now embrace capitalism, and now have an increase in inequality that they are unwilling to address. In fairness, the SCO has developed some plans to counter some of the key global challenges; however, instead of being leaders that aim to counter all the global challenges, they are more interested in adding to the World of Disorder at a time when the world least needs it.

Moises Naim states that we now live in the 'more revolution', which describes a world of abundance, and that we now need to address so many challenges that it has become difficult for any one nation to fix.[156] Hence, it is necessary for democratic nations to form an international organisation that provides yearly updates on the work being carried out to address the seven key global challenges. If people in democratic nations believe democracy has failed because so many challenges have emerged, and that the autocratic worldview put forward by China and Russia is the answer, then I disagree. The autocratic SCO and nations like Russia and China are not interested in solving the world's problems, but are more interested in gaining power for power's sake. For China and Russia it is like a *Game of Thrones*, and when President Jinping is 65 years old and President Putin is 66 years old they want to fight hard over the next decade to gain global power and dominance and be on the Iron Throne. Instead, the world needs to unite to fight the common enemy of climate change that affects all people and all nations now, as well as the six other key challenges.

The road ahead is hard but we must fight against fear itself and aim to defeat and overcome the seven key challenges for the benefit of humanity. To do so we must form an international organisation like a Republic Earth Organisation to coordinate a global response to each threat. Republic Earth aims to rally people to protect Mother Earth from the threat of humanity's extinction. It aims to encourage young people especially to join one or all of the fights to counter the challenges. This book does not have all the answers but it offers a framework of what is needed to be done, especially by democratic nations to overcome the growing World of Disorder. At the same time that we are building a global society and a new World of Order, we must use the global community to overcome the World of Disorder.

Now, let us learn more about the seven key global challenges and look at some initial ideas to address each threat.

CHAPTER 16: CLIMATE CHANGE THREATS

The most significant threat that humanity faces in the 21st century is climate change. Both the Republic Earth Organisation and the SCO are committed to addressing this threat; however, democratic nations rather than autocratic nations are leading these efforts. On 12 December 2015, the Paris Agreement was agreed to within the United Nations Framework Convention on Climate Change (UNFCCC), dealing with greenhouse gas emissions, mitigation, adaptation, and finance, starting in 2020.[157]

As of July 2018, 195 UNFCCC members have signed the agreement, and 179 have become party to it.[158] However, on 4 August 2017, US President Donald Trump delivered an official notice to the UN that the US intends to withdraw from the Paris Agreement as soon as it is legal to do so.[159] This means the US is seeking to withdraw from the global leadership role of addressing the most significant challenge facing humanity, which is deeply disappointing. The US is the world's second-biggest emitter of carbon dioxide, and a pact without the powerhouse nation is significantly weakened. The Paris Agreement is also not legally binding and it is unenforceable.

The Paris Agreement's long-term goal is to keep the increase in global average temperatures to well below two per cent above pre-industrial levels, and to limit the increase to 1.5 per cent, since this would substantially reduce the risks and effects of climate change.[160] We need to act in a global response to address the increase in the climate change threats that we face.

In 2017, Mexico broke its annual temperature record for the fourth consecutive year. On 27 January 2017, the temperature reached 43.4°C at Puerto Madryn, Argentina—the highest temperature recorded so far south (43°S) anywhere in the world.[161] On 28 May 2017, in Turbat, western Pakistan, the high of 53.5°C tied Pakistan's all-time highest temperature and became the world-record highest temperature for May.[162] In the Arctic, the 2017 land surface temperature was 1.6°C above the

1981–2010 average; the second highest since the record began in 1900, behind only 2016.[163] The five highest annual Arctic temperatures have all occurred since 2007.[164]

In the tropics, 2017 saw 85 named tropical storms, slightly above the 1981–2010 average of 82.[165] The North Atlantic basin was the only basin that featured an above-normal season; its seventh most active in the 164-year record.[166] Three hurricanes in the basin were especially notable. Harvey produced record rainfall totals in areas of Texas and Louisiana, including a storm total of 1538.7 mm near Beaumont, Texas, which far exceeds the previous known US tropical cyclone record of 1320.8 mm.[167] Irma was the strongest tropical cyclone globally in 2017 and the strongest Atlantic hurricane outside of the Gulf of Mexico and Caribbean on record, with maximum winds of 295 km h−1.[168] Maria caused catastrophic destruction across the Caribbean islands, including devastating wind damage and flooding across Puerto Rico with more than 3,000 deaths.[169]

Among noteworthy regional precipitation records in 2017, Russia reported its second wettest year on record (after 2013) and Norway experienced its sixth wettest year since records began in 1900.[170] Across India, heavy rain and flood-related incidents during the monsoon season claimed around 800 lives.[171] In August and September, above-normal precipitation triggered the most devastating floods in more than a decade in the Venezuelan states of Bolívar and Delta Amacuro.[172] In Nigeria, heavy rain during August and September caused the Niger and Benue rivers to overflow, bringing floods that displaced more than 100,000 people.[173]

In the US, an extreme western wildfire season burned over 4 million hectares; the total costs of $18 billion tripled the previous US annual wildfire cost record set in 1991.[174]

In India, where 24 cities are expected to reach average summertime highs of at least 35°C (95°F) by 2050, it is the slum dwellers who are most vulnerable.[175] And as the global risk of prolonged exposure to deadly heat steadily rises, so do the associated risks of human catastrophe.

In 2018, deadly fires scorched swathes of the Northern Hemisphere, from California to Arctic Sweden and down to Greece on the sunny Mediterranean.[176] Drought in Europe has turned verdant land barren, while people in Japan and Korea are dying from record-breaking heat.[177]

Climate change is here and is affecting the entire globe—not just the polar bears or tiny islands vulnerable to rising sea levels—scientists say. It is on the doorsteps of everyday Americans, Europeans and Asians, and the best evidence shows it will get much worse.

In 2018, 119 people in Japan died in a heatwave, while 29 were killed in South Korea, officials there say.[178] Ninety-one people in Greece died in wildfires, and fires in California took at least 88 lives.[179] Spain and Portugal sweltered through an exceptionally hot weekend with a heatwave that killed three people in Spain and pushed temperatures toward record levels.[180]

Deadly heatwaves will become more frequent and occur in more places on the planet in coming decades, according to a study published in the journal *Nature Climate Change*. Extreme heatwaves are frequently cited as one of the most direct effects of man-made climate change.

A report released by the US National Oceanic and Atmospheric Administration (NOAA) gave the Earth in 2017 a grim report card by stating that, 'the major greenhouse gases—carbon dioxide, methane and nitrous oxide—all rose to record levels last year. The global average carbon dioxide concentration was the highest ever recorded, and higher than at any point in the past 800,000 years, according to ice-core data'.[181] The global growth rate of CO2 has nearly quadrupled since the early 1960s.

Unfortunately, spending on oil and gas increased last year, pushing up the share of fossil fuels in energy supply investment for the first time since 2014, according to the International Energy Agency.[182] Investment in renewable energy dropped seven per cent, while demand for coal rose, largely to keep Asia's furnaces burning as the region rapidly develops.[183]

Meanwhile, last year a new record for global sea levels was set.[184] Unprecedented coral bleaching occurred, and both the Arctic and the Antarctic saw record low levels of sea ice, as warmer air and seas continued the trend of thinning out the polar ice.[185]

In July 2018, we witnessed floods and a heatwave in Japan, wildfires in Greece, Sweden and California. In August 2018, according to Jen Mills, 'the heatwave gripping large stretches of Europe has already been blamed for deadly forest fires and crop failures. Now, freshwater fish could be its next victims. Some regions in Germany sweltered as the mercury hit 39°C. Rivers like the Rhine and the Elbe have soaked up so much heat that fish are beginning to suffocate. "I'm expecting a tragedy as soon as next week," Philipp Sicher from the Swiss Fishery Association told German news agency dpa. In Hamburg, authorities collected almost five metric tonnes of dead fish from ponds over the weekend, dpa reported. Firefighters have started pumping fresh water into some ponds and lakes in a bid to raise oxygen levels. Scientists say the record heat seen in Europe, North America and parts of Asia this year points to the influence of man-made climate change, and could become more common in future.'[186]

2018 was one of the hottest years since records began, with unprecedented peak temperatures engulfing the planet, from 43°C (109°F) in Baku, Azerbaijan, to the low 30s across Scandinavia.[187] In Kyoto, Japan, the mercury did not dip below 38°C (100°F) for a week.[188] In the US, an unusually early and humid July heatwave saw 48.8°C (120°F) in Chino, inland of Los Angeles. Residents blasted their air-conditioners so much they caused power shortages.[189]

Urban areas are reaching these killer temperatures faster than those that are less populated. Cities absorb, create and radiate heat. Asphalt, brick, concrete and dark roofs act like sponges for heat during the day and emit warmth at night. Air-conditioning is a lifesaver for those who can afford it, but it makes the streets even hotter for those who can't.

The World Health Organization says that 68 per cent of people will live in cities by 2050, and the more densely populated they become, the hotter they'll get.[190] Considering that recent predictions warn temperatures in South Asia will exceed the limits of human survival by the end of the century, every degree counts.[191] Even this year, 65 people have perished from nearly 44°C (111°F) heat in Karachi, Pakistan—a city used to extreme heat.[192]

Last year, Hawaiian researchers projected that the share of the world's population exposed to deadly heat for at least 20 days a year will increase from 30 per cent now to 74 per cent by 2100 if greenhouse gas emissions are allowed to grow. (It will rise to 48 per cent with 'drastic reductions'.)[193] They concluded that, 'an increasing threat to human life from excess heat now seems almost inevitable'.[194]

'Dying in a heatwave is like being slowly cooked,' said lead author Professor Camilo Mora at the time of publication.[195] 'It's pure torture. The young and elderly are at particular risk, but we found that this heat can kill soldiers, athletes, everyone.'[196]

While climate scientists have long argued that you can't attribute any single weather event to climate change, a study last year by the National Academies of Sciences, Engineering and Medicine concluded: 'The science has advanced to the point that this is no longer true as an unqualified blanket statement. In many cases, it is now often possible to make and defend quantitative statements about the extent to which human-induced climate change ... has influenced either the magnitude or the probability of occurrence of specific types of events or event classes.'[197] Climate change makes the hots hotter, the wets wetter and the dries drier.

Heidi Cullen, chief scientist for Climate Central, an environmental organisation, was quoted as telling the Weather Channel in July 2018 that the national academies' report connecting global warming to the increased risk and severity of certain classes of extreme weather—like some of the heatwaves, floods and droughts we're experiencing—carries the same scientific import as the US surgeon general's 1964 report connecting smoking to lung cancer.[198] According to Thomas Friedman, 'In other words: Mother Nature is done letting us pretend that we don't know and can't connect the dots—and that could create some very interesting politics.'[199]

According to Thomas Friedman, 'There are currently 7.6 billion people on the planet, and in 2030 there will be 8.6 billion—another one billion in just over a decade! If even half of them get cars, have air-conditioners and eat high-protein diets like Americans now do, we will devour and burn up the planet beyond recognition. So what does that mean? It means clean energy and efficiency have to be the next great global industry or we're going to be a bad biological experiment, whether there is climate change or not. Does anyone—other than Trump—believe that America can continue to dominate the world economy and not lead the next great global industry, but leave that to China? Clean power, clean cars, clean manufacturing and efficient buildings make everything we want to achieve in our society easier.'[200]

The Republic Earth Organisation has a global agenda. Climate change may be far beyond the concerns of some, but according to Yuval Harari, 'it might eventually make the Mumbai slums inhabitable, send enormous new waves of refugees across the Mediterranean, and lead to a worldwide crisis in healthcare', and thus we need to address this great challenge to humanity now.[201]

The Republic Earth Organisation is deeply disappointed that on the third anniversary of the Paris Agreement, the Trump Administration marked it by working with Russia and the Gulf oil nations to sideline science and undermine the accord at the climate talks in Poland. The US needs to be a leader in the fight against climate change, especially when it is affected by natural disasters. According to former Secretary of State John Kerry, 'Fifteen of the biggest fires in California history have occurred in the past 18 years ... Hurricanes Maria, Harvey and Irma cost the United States some $265 billion in damages. Historic droughts are matched by historic floods. Heatwaves stole 153 billion hours of labor globally last years. Infectious diseases are moving into new areas and higher altitudes. Crop yields are down in more than two dozen countries, and by 2050 the Midwestern United States could see agricultural productivity drop to its lowest level in decades. The latest report by the Intergovernmental Panel on Climate Change warned that the changes required to hold global warming to 2.7 degrees Fahrenheit or 1.5 degrees Celsius, as called for in the Paris Agreement, would require changes on a scale with "no documented historic precedent". Even the recent congressional mandated climate assessment warns that "with continued growth in emissions at historic rates, annual losses in some economic sectors are projected to reach hundreds of billions of dollars by the end of the century—more than the current gross domestic product of any US States".'[202]

The Republic Earth Organisation agrees with the World Wildlife Fund's 2018 *Living Planet Report* that a new global deal for nature and people is urgently needed and we must begin the project in 2019. Everything that has built modern human society is provided by nature and, increasingly, research demonstrates the natural world's incalculable importance to our health, wealth, food and security. According to the WWF report, 'While climate change is a growing threat, the main drivers of biodiversity decline continue to be the overexploitation of species, agriculture and land conversion. Indeed, a recent assessment found that only a quarter of land on Earth is substantively free of impacts of human activities. This is projected to decline to just one tenth by 2050 ... Marine and freshwater ecosystems are also facing huge pressures. Almost 6 billion tonnes of fish and invertebrates have been taken from the world's oceans since 1950. Plastic pollution has been detected in all major marine environments worldwide, from shorelines and surface waters down to the deepest parts of the ocean, including the bottom of the Mariana Trench. The Living Planet Index also tracks the state of global biodiversity by measuring the population abundance of thousands of vertebrate species around the world. The latest index shows an overall decline of 60 per cent in population sizes between 1970 and 2014.'[203]

The Republic Earth Organisation is deeply concerned with the facts outlined above, but is pleased that the WWF is collaborating with a consortium of almost 40 universities and conservation and intergovernmental organisations to launch the research initiative bending the curve of biodiversity loss.[204] We would also like to see nations around the world commit half of the planet to nature, as only by doing so can we save the immensity of life forms. The worry is that unless humanity learns a great deal more about biodiversity and moves quickly to protect it, we will soon lose most of the species composing life on Earth.

There is no part of the world that is not affected by climate change, and thus all nations need to work collectively to combat it. In 2019, post the Election we hope the Australian Labor Party in Australia will continue to tackle climate change from Opposition, but more demo-cratic nations are needed to lead the change as well. Unfortunately, autocratic member nations of the SCO in Russia and Iran do not appear to be interested in taking action when many people in their nations want action to be taken. The threat posed by climate change is nothing that humanity has faced before and nations will need to increasingly work together to make sure that by 2030 we are making progress. It is vital that a Republic Earth Organisation is created to coordinate these efforts, so that by 2030 we are helping protect future generations from the growing dangers of climate change.

CHAPTER 17: INEQUALITY

One of the key challenges in the World of Disorder is an increase in global economic inequality, where the top one per cent own more than half the world's wealth.[205] In every country you can witness this inequality. We are also witnessing a reduction in global poverty levels and an increase in the global middle class, which is welcomed. However, over the last 19 years there has been an increase in global inequality that needs to be addressed. We need to achieve a fairer global society. The wages of the rich elite continue to increase whereas wages for the middle class have barely moved.[206] While global productivity has grown, the benefits are flowing to firms and their owners, not to workers. Moreover, we have witnessed over the last 40 years a massive transfer of power away from governments and into the hands of major corporations, leading to an increase in inequality. Take, for example, the taxi industry, which was controlled and regulated by governments around the world. Now, with the rise of Uber and other companies, the taxi industry has lost its market share and power has transferred away from the governments and into the private companies, which are often not fully regulated, often don't pay adequate taxes and often don't pay their drivers well either, which leads to an increase in inequality.

The SCO is not fully committed to tackling inequality. In China and Russia we are witnessing an increase in inequality, which is interesting in light of their communist pasts. In terms of China, the Bloomberg Billionaires Index tracks the wealth of the 500 richest individuals globally, 38 of whom are Chinese.[207] More broadly, global wealth research firm Wealth X found that of the world's 2,754 billionaires, 338 were in China (12 per cent).[208] UBS Group AG estimates that a new billionaire is minted in China every two days.[209] In terms of Russia, the richest 10 per cent own 87 per cent of all the country's wealth, which means Russia is rated as the most unequal of the world's major economies.[210] From the outside, both the Chinese and Russian governments do not appear to be interested in tackling either inequality domestically or globally, and thus the rich get richer and the poor get poorer.

In Australia, we also have our problems. Australia is among countries with the highest growth in income inequality in the world over the past 30 years, according to the International Monetary Fund.[211] Just the top two billionaires in Australia now have about as much wealth as the bottom fifth of the population.[212] In Australia, it is hoped that post the 2019 Election that Labor can again from Opposition start to tackle the problem of inequality and create a fairer society, which is what Australia is known for and is one of our great strengths as a nation.

The Republic Earth Organisation is extremely worried about the increase in inequality, as the 21st century might represent the most unequal society in history. According to Yuval Harari, 'by 2100, the richest 1 per cent might own not merely most of the world's wealth, but also most of the world's beauty, creativity and health. The two processes together—bioengineering coupled with the rise of AI—might therefore result in the separation of human kind into a small class of super humans and massive underclass'.[213] We must ensure that the forces of globalisation, the digital revolution, biotech advances and AI advances do not create a more unequal global society.

The Republic Earth Organisation believes we need to civilise capitalism and ensure we create new jobs with great working conditions that unions and governments monitor to ensure the global society can succeed. For example, if we regulate the AI revolution, we can make sure that AI does not take away people's jobs unnecessarily. We should be working on ways to cut costs of living and not people's jobs, their wealth and their quality of life. Republic Earth, as mentioned earlier, is about a new way of looking at the world and creating a fairer and more just society.

We believe that to overcome the growing trend of economic inequality we should embrace Thomas Piketty's idea of a global progressive tax on capital coupled with a high level of international financial transparency, as outlined in his book *Capital: In the Twenty-First Century*. According to Piketty, 'The primary purpose of the capital tax is not finance the social state but to regulate capitalism. The goal is first to stop the indefinite increase of inequality of wealth, and second to impose effective regulation on the financial and banking system in order to avoid crisis. To achieve these two ends, the capital tax must first promote democratic and financial transparency: there should be clarity about who owns what assets around the world.'[214] Thus, to contain the unlimited growth of inequality of wealth, a capital tax schedule with rates of 0.1 or 0.5 per cent on fortunes under AU S$1 million; 1 per cent on fortunes between AU S$1 million and AU S$5 million, 2 per cent between AU S$5 million and AU S$10 million; and between 5 per cent and 10 per cent of several hundred million or several billion Australian dollars should be implemented.

'Extreme poverty vs extreme wealth: how big is the inequality gap?

1. Boomtime for the world's billionaires. It is 10 years since the financial crisis that shook our world and caused enormous suffering. In that time, the fortunes of the richest have risen dramatically. The number of billionaires has almost doubled, with a new billionaire created every two days between 2017 and 2018. They have now more wealth than ever before while almost half of humanity have barely escaped extreme poverty, living on less than $5.50 a day.

LAST YEAR 26 PEOPLE OWNED THE SAME AS THE 3.8 BILLION PEOPLE WHO MAKE UP THE POOREST HALF OF HUMANITY.

2. Wealth undertaxed. While the richest continue to enjoy booming fortunes, they are also enjoying some of the lowest levels of tax in decades—as are the corporations that they own. Instead taxes are falling disproportionately on working people. When governments undertax the rich, there's less money for vital services like healthcare and education, increasing inequality and poverty.

3. Underfunded public services. At the same time, public services are suffering from chronic underfunding or being outsourced to private companies that exclude the poorest people. In many countries a decent education or quality healthcare has become a luxury only the rich can afford. It has profound implications for the future of our children and the opportunities they will have to live a better and longer life.

4. Denied a longer life. In most countries having money is a passport to better health and a longer life, while being poor all too often means more sickness and an earlier grave. People from poor communities can expect to die ten or twenty years earlier than people in wealthy areas. In developing countries, a child from a poor family is twice as likely to die before the age of five than a child from a rich family.

5. Inequality is sexist. We all suffer when public services are neglected, but women and girls pay the highest price. Girls are pulled out of school first when the money isn't available to pay fees, and women clock up hours looking after sick relatives when healthcare systems fail. Most profoundly, our economic prosperity is dependent on the huge but unrecognized contribution made by women through unpaid care work.'[215]

The Republic Earth Organisation is really concerned about inequality in all countries, and we need to change the rules. Take the US, for example, where nearly one in four can't pay their bills on time; a lower proportion of Americans own their homes than at any time in the past half century—63.5 per cent; and nearly one-third of the population—76 million—describe themselves as either struggling to get by or just getting by.[216] Incomes have either been reduced or are stagnating, while expenses keep going up. We need to change these rules as incomes should be increasing and expenses should be decreasing to reduce inequality.

In August 2018, US Senator Elizabeth Warren led efforts to not only better protect the US middle class by proposing a new Federal Bill called the Accountable Capitalism Act, but was also better protecting the global middle class.[217] The aim of the bill is to redistribute trillions of dollars from rich executives and shareholders to the middle class without costing a dollar. The Republic Earth Organisation would aim to encourage member nations to pass similar acts in their own nations.

We want all peoples and all nations to enjoy the benefits of the global middle class and avoid the effects of inequality. We understand that despite the concerns of the rich, regulations work and can have a massive impact on reducing inequality and creating a fairer global society. It is vital that the world builds a new model to ensure a fair and more equal global society is created for all.

CHAPTER 18: TERRORISM
and CYBERTERRORISM

One of the great challenges in the growing World of Disorder has been the threat posed by terrorism and cyberterrorism. Over the last 19 years there has been an increase in both. In 2017, over 11,000 terrorist attacks occurred in more than 100 countries, and every day nations, businesses and ordinary people are targeted by a wide variety of cyber-attacks.[218] Despite efforts to target terrorist groups and cyber crimi-nals, the threat continues to increase, and thus a coordinated global response is needed to reduce these threats.

Through the formation of a new global democratic organisation, like Republic Earth Organisation, we should work to develop policies to counter both terrorism and cyberterrorism. Democratic nations have worked well to counter the threat posed by Islamic State (ISIL), and entities like the Five Eyes (US, UK, Canada, Australia and New Zealand) work well to counter cyberterrorists; however, a lot more work is need-ed. Autocratic nations like Russia have suffered from a range of terror-ist attacks, including from Islamic State, and are addressing the threat of terrorism. However, autocratic nations are actually also responsible for cyberterrorism, especially at the expense of democratic nations. Democratic nations should stay well clear of entities like the SCO when its member nations are actually contributing to the World of Disorder by carrying out cyberattacks on nations, businesses and people. In the next decade we, as democratic nations, need to get into a war like footing to counter the threats of terrorism and cyberterrorism, as we have the ability to radically reduce both.

i   Terrorism

Terrorism is both a global political problem and an internal psychologi-cal mechanism. Terrorism 'works by pressing the fear button deep in our minds and hijacking the private imagination of millions of individu-als'.[219] There are many different terrorist groups who carry out attacks around the world, with many different political agendas, but the key is to strengthen the global middle class so as to reduce the risk of people being enticed to join terrorist groups and carry out these acts of violence. This solution may not prevent terrorism but it will help, and we must do all we can to reduce the risk of terrorism. We must encourage people who are upset with the status quo to rebel in a peaceful, democratic manner and not to carry out acts of violence to achieve their political agenda.

Terrorism is usually understood to be the use or threat of violence to further a political cause, and over the next decade we must educate people living in the emerging global society that no political agenda should use violence. Where people live in autocratic regimes and they cannot speak out in dissent in fear of being imprisoned, we must redouble our efforts to help in such situations, to demand peacefully that a democratic society be created so their voices can be heard. Democratic societies allow grievances to be heard, and this is the greatness of democracy. We must do all we can to continue to protect our democratic way of life, but terrorism our recent years has played a role in threatening this way of life, and we must redouble our efforts to curb it at all costs.

There are many different types of terrorist groups but the main threat in the 21st century has come from fundamentalist terrorism, not only in the form of groups like al-Qaeda and the Islamic State, but also alt-right wing white supremacist fundamentalists. In countries like Australia, both forms of fundamentalist terrorism are on the rise and we must do all we can to counter the threat.

The terror attacks of 11 September 2001, known as 9/11, marked a turning point in world history and the beginning of the 'War on Terror'.[220] The attacks are estimated to have killed 3,000 people, making it the deadliest terrorist incident in human history. The subsequent War on Terror led to the invasion of Afghanistan in 2001 and Iraq in 2003. More than a quarter of all terrorist attacks between 9/11 and 2008 took place in Iraq.[221]

In 2015 in terms of terror attacks, the following major ones took place: 224 people died when Russian Metrojet Flight 9268 was destroyed by a bomb above Sinai, Egypt; 137 died in the November terror attacks in Paris, France.[222] In 2016, more than 50 died in the Zliten truck bombing in Libya; more than 63 died in the Al-Shabaab terrorist attack on an African Union Kenya Army Base in Somalia; 35 died in two suicide bombings in Brussels Airport and one on Brussels Metro; 70 died in the Lahore suicide bombing in Pakistan; 49 died in a mass shooting at a nightclub in Orlando, US; 45 died in a terrorist attack at Ataturk Airport in Istanbul, Turkey; 87 died during the Bastille Day attack in Nice, France; 12 died in the Berlin attack, Germany, in the lead up to Christmas.[223] In 2017, 36 died at a Shia market in Baghdad; 88 died in the Sehwan suicide bombing in Pakistan; 40 died in an attack on a military hospital in Kabul, Afghanistan; 47 died during the Palm Sunday Christian church bombings in Egypt; five died in a suicide bombing on the St Petersburg metro in Russia; 22 died in the Manchester Arena bombing in the UK; 11 died in the London Bridge attack in the UK; 22 died in the Tehran terrorist attacks in Iran; 15 people died in the Barcelona terrorist attacks in Spain; and eight died in the Lower Manhattan terrorist attacks in the US.[224]

In 2018, 103 died in the Kabul ambulance bombing in Afghanistan; 45 died in the Mogadishu attacks, Somalia; 86 died in the Mubi suicide bombings, Nigeria; five died in the Carcassonne and Trebes attacks, France; 25 died in the Surabaya bombings, Indonesia; 16 died on the High National Elections Commission in Tripoli, Libya; four died in the Liege attack, Belgium; 154 died in the 13 July 2018 Pakistan bombings; 255 died in the As-Suwayda terrorist attack, Syria; and 118 died in the Borno State attack, Nigeria.[225] This is just a small list of some recent terrorist attacks around the world. While most have taken place in the Middle East, the threat posed by terrorism is a global problem and over the last 19 years it has only increased.

Most of these attacks occurred as a form of jihadi terrorism, which over the years has been inspired by Osama bin Laden's brand of terrorism from groups like al-Qaeda and its various off-shoots like Islamic State. According to Ali Soufan, 'Whereas on 9/11 al-Qaeda had around 400 members, today it has thousands upon thousands, in franchises and affiliates spread from the shores of the Pacific to Africa's Atlantic seaboard—and that is without even counting the breakaway armed group that calls itself Islamic State. Al-Qaeda's Syrian branch alone has more members than bin Laden ever imagined for his entire network ... In the Middle East, Islamic State, al-Qaeda's most vicious off-shoot to date, employs methods so savage that even hardened terrorists publicly denounce their brutality. Where bin Laden encouraged militants in his network to focus on attacking the West directly rather than hitting regimes in the Muslim world, the Islamic State has successfully done both. It has brought mass murder to the streets of Paris, airports in Brussels and Istanbul, a Russian airliner in the skies over Sinai, and a Christmas market in Berlin. It has killed worshipers at mosques in Yemen and Kuwait, attacked police, soldiers, and border guards in Egypt and Saudi Arabia, and bombed political rallies in Turkey.'[226]

One of the key problems is that al-Qaeda has successfully peddled the view that democratic nations, or the West, is engaged in a 'war against Islam'. According to Ali Soufan, 'This opinion is by no means confined to a handful of extremists. On the contrary, millions of Muslims around the world believe the West is deliberately suppressing their religion and stifling political change in order to keep repressive secular governments in power. Unfortunately, almost nothing is being done to counter this impression; giving jihadis free rein to exploit the misconception for their own needs ... How can we begin to counter such messages? How do we cauterize the wounds from which extremism grows? First, we must expose the basic hypocrisy of a movement that claims to be the arbiter of true Islamic piety yet routinely bombs mosques—including, in 2016, the second holiest in the world, the Prophet's Mosque in Medina, a site visited by millions of Muslim pilgrims every year, particularly during the month of Ramadan, when the Islamic State chose to strike. While we are laying bare the lies, we must craft a true story to drown out the false ones terrorists tell. It is not a question of trying to match jihadi claims tit for tat with bare denials, but of creating an entirely new narrative—ideally one with even greater appeal, because it is based not on lies and despair but on truth and hope. Such a story has the potential to push thousands of young off the treadmill of radicalization before it carries them into the jihadi echo chamber. But the narrative will only succeed if it is tailored, like that of the terrorists, not just from country to country but down to the level of different groups and communities.'[227]

Republic Earth Organisation

The Republic Earth Organisation wants to work on countering violent extremism strategies so that a new narrative like the one proposed by Ali Soufan can grow and provide a new hope for the world and at the same time reduce the terrorist threat.

The internet has become a central tool for terrorists, largely replacing print and other physical media. It has allowed terrorist organisations to costlessly communicate their messages and aims to the world, allowing them to recruit new members, coordinate global attacks and better evade surveillance. The terrorist group known as the Islamic State (also, ISIS and ISIL) is arguably the first to harness the power of the internet and social media. Their well-organised online propaganda campaign has seen them recruit thousands of foreign fighters. The Republic Earth Organisation believes we must do all we can to undermine the power of terrorist groups' online presence on the internet and disrupt their activities.

In Australia, we have suffered from our own terrorist attacks. It began on 23 September 2014 when a young man tried to kill two police officers after a fatwa was issued by Islamic State, by stabbing them to death outside the Endeavour Hills Police Station.[228] As a result of this attack and many others around the world, Australia has become a key member of the international military intervention against Islamic State. Australia has suffered a series of attacks since the Endeavour Hills incident, including the Sydney hostage crisis in 2014 when three people died; one person died in the 2015 Parramatta shooting; one person died during the Brighton siege of 2017; and one person died during the Melbourne stabbing attack in 2018.[229]

In response, Australia has also legislated new national security laws to better protect us and deal with the threats of terrorism and cyberterrorism, which include: Counter Terrorism Legislation Amendment Bill 2018; Home Affairs and Integrity Agencies Legislation Amendment Bill 2018; Identity-matching Services Bill 2018 and the Australian Passports Amendment (Identity-matching Services) Bill 2018; reviewing the Office of National Intelligence Bill 2018; Police stop, search and seizure powers, the control order regime and the preventative detention order regime; Criminal Code Amendment (High Risk Terrorist Offenders) Bill

2016; Telecommunications (Interception and Access) Amendment (Data Retention) Bill 2014; Counter Terrorism Legislation Amendment (Foreign Fighters) Bill 2014; National Security Legislation Amendment Bill 2014; and the Office of National Intelligence (Consequential and Transitional Provisions) Bill 2018; and reviewing the Crimes Legislation Amendment (Police Powers at Airports) Bill 2018.[230] These new national security laws have made a real difference and have helped to make Australia safer.

It is true that acts of terrorism still account for much fewer global deaths than those from cancers, but the threat posed by terrorism is still a major concern.[231] The Republic Earth Organisation believes we must do all we can to pursue a global response to prevent a further increase in terrorist attacks around the world.

ii   Cyberterrorism

In recent years, an alarming rise in the incidence of cyberattacks has made cyber security a major concern for nations across the globe. In addition to tackling terrorism, the Republic Earth Organisation believes we need a global response amongst democratic nations to tackle cyberterrorism. Unfortunately, the SCO is not interested in tackling cyberterrorism on a global scale, and instead its leading member nations, China and Russia, carry out state-sponsored cyberattacks against democratic nations. The Republic Earth Organisation believes the SCO is not fit to put forward new global plans for the world when its leading member nations are actually adding to the World of Disorder by carrying out these attacks. The world faces not only state-sponsored cyberattacks but also cyberattacks from hackers, terrorist groups and other third parties.

There have been some major state-sponsored cyberattacks carried out by both China and Russia. For example, Chinese hackers breached Google's corporate servers and gained access to classified information back in 2009, while in 2014 a six-month-long cyberattack took place on the German parliament by the Russian Sofacy Group.[232] Other major cyberattacks have included a state-sponsored attack on Yahoo in 2013-14, affecting 3 billion account users; between 2014-18, 500 million Marriot

105

customers had their data stolen by a Chinese intelligence group; while between 2012-14 personal information of 22 million current and former employees of the US Office of Personal Management where stolen by hackers from China.[233]

Cyberattacks are now affecting every country. In 2018, for example, up to 400 Australian businesses may have been targeted by suspected Russian state-sponsored cyberattacks that have affected millions of machines worldwide.[234] In all of these cases the founding nations of the SCO—China and Russia—have been responsible, and it appears that all they are interested in is bullying and stealing power away from democratic nations, corporations and governments operating in democracies. The Republic Earth Organisation believes democratic nations need to fight back and expose the wrongdoing by these countries.

We are extremely worried about the prospects of cyberattacks, surveillance and AI in the future, and democratic nations should work together to protect citizens from the harmful effects of them. For example, according to Yuval Harari, 'Consider surveillance. Numerous countries around the world, including several democracies, are busy building unprecedented systems of surveillance. For example, Israel is a leader in the field of surveillance technology, and has created in the occupied West Bank a working prototype for a total-surveillance regime...It therefore takes surprisingly few Israeli soldiers to effectively control the roughly 2.5 million Palestinians who live in the West Bank...What Palestinians are experiencing today in the West Bank may be just a primitive preview of what billions of people will eventually experience all over the planet.'[235]

The Republic Earth Organisation is concerned about this future and the prospects that leading nations of the SCO will develop a global total surveillance system of everyone on the planet, which will infringe people's human rights and privacy, and which will be difficult to counter. We must ensure that these nations not only do not get control of the world's data and the digital revolution, but we must also protect citizens from a grim future of an increase in cyberattacks, surveillance and AI wreaking harm around the world. We believe we need to unite democratic peoples and nations to better protect the citizens of the world, not only from terrorism but also from cyberterrorism to ensure the global society can succeed in the 21st century.

CHAPTER 19: DISPLACED PEOPLE AND REFUGEES

One of the key challenges in the World of Disorder has been the rapid increase in displaced people and refugees around the world. In 2018, there were around 250 million people on the move. The United Nations Refugee Agency said there was a record-high 68 million migrants, including 25 million refugees, wandering the world in 2018.[236] When responding to this challenge, some nations have become more nationalistic and have reduced refugee intakes or used the idea of building a wall to stem the flow of displaced people and refugees. The problem with reducing refugee intakes or building a wall is that it denies the bigger problem in that humanity has never faced so many people being on the move at the same time. These people need to go somewhere and if they cannot get into one country then other nations face the burden of dealing with too many refugees. We understand that globally many people are concerned about the threat of refugees, and right-wing or conservative governments have successfully played on people's fears. However, no one country has offered a successful global solution to stem the tide of refugees as it continues to grow as a problem, and many nations like the US and Australia have pursued nationalistic policies in their respective countries.

In 2018, the list of refugee emergencies increased. In terms of the Syrian Regional Refugee response, over 5.6 million refugees have fled Syria since 2011, seeking safety in Turkey, Lebanon, Jordan, Iraq, Egypt and beyond.[237] There are refugee emergencies in South Sudan, Central African Republic (1 million have fled since 2013), the Democratic Republic of Congo (100,000 fled to neighbouring countries in 2017), Somalia, Mali, Nigeria, El Salvador, Guatemala, Honduras, Yemen, Burundi, Iraq, Mozambique, Myanmar (738,000 refugees have fled Myanmar to Bangladesh since August 2017), Ukraine and Venezuela (more than 1.5 million people fled in 2017 and more fled in 2018).[238]

We now have a record 59 refugee camps around the world.[239] Millions from South America and Central America want to go to the US, and over

1 million from both Syria and Africa fled to Europe in 2015, with more continuing to leave on a daily basis.[240] Citizens around the world, worried about the increase, are asking political leaders to act. The problem is that nations are carrying out national policies to a global problem, and we believe only a global solution can stem the tide. If we do not act soon, the number of refugees and displaced people will increase.

In the Sahel region between Senegal and Somalia, once fertile land is drying out because of climate change, and people are on the move.[241] There are over 60 million people living in the Sahel region and if the majority go on the move in the coming years this will only double the problem.[242] Even a World Bank study predicated that further climate change would displaced as many as 143 million from Africa, South Asia, and Latin America by 2050.[243] We also have many economic migrants leaving unsafe or poorer parts of the world to seek a better life elsewhere. This is a key challenge in the World of Disorder and we must act quickly to provide a global response to prevent a further increase in the numbers of displaced people and refugees.

The SCO is not leading the way in dealing with this challenge. Both China and Russia believe they have too many domestic issues to be able to take on a leading role in dealing with this global issue. Today, China has no refugee resettlement policy or national legislation on asylum.[244] Chinese officials merely acknowledged the humanitarian crisis in neighbouring Myanmar, and opted not to shelter Syrians escaping a multi-year war.[245] While in Russia, as of 1 July 2018, there are some 2,650 refugees, which is an extremely small amount for a nation wanting a large role in world affairs.[246] Whereas in Australia, even under a Coalition Conservative Government, we have had more than 24,000 humanitarian arrivals settled in the past financial year.[247]

The Republic Earth Organisation believes we need to establish a Global Migration Organisation and that democratic nations need to be on the front foot, as they are at present, in dealing with this problem. It is pleasing that the United Nations invited member nations to an Intergovernmental Conference to Adopt the Global Compact for Safe, Orderly and Regular Migration in Marrakech, Morocco, on 10-11 December 2018.[248] As mentioned earlier, this Global Compact sets out a common understanding, shared responsibilities and unity of purpose regarding migration. In light of this agreement, we desperately need to create a Global Migration Organisation to deal with the increase in displaced people and refugees.

One plan being considered by the Republic Earth Organisation is to set up a better system of managing refugee camps around the world with UNICEF. The goal would be to invite democratic nations to take responsibility for a camp, or work with other nations to jointly fund and manage refugee camps. Each refugee camp would have certain basic requirements to offer a school, jobs and housing until a safe country can be found to call home. In addition, anyone trying to travel illegally would be sent back or sent to one of the refugee camps managed by this nation. This plan would aim to reduce illegal arrivals of refugees, which has become a major issue in the 21st century.

This plan would also ensure refugees are treated with a higher standard of care and are provided with the dignity of children going to school and the opportunity to work within the camp. Some may argue against providing a high standard of care for refugees, but we need to ensure all citizens have access to a good education, and obtain skills to acquire a job and join the global middle class.

The plan under the Republic Earth Organisation is that, unlike the SCO, we are keen to fully address the increase in displaced people and refugees. It is vital we work to increase the number of people entering the global middle class and thus work with nations to ensure people in every country enjoy a great quality of life. We want poorer, still developing countries to become developed countries; however, in many cases climate change or war or conflict is forcing people to flee. Accordingly, the Republic Earth Organisation believes the creation of a Global Migration Organisation working with the UNHCR can better manage the problem at hand.

CHAPTER 20: HARM CAUSED BY
THE DIGITAL REVOLUTION

One of the key challenges to address is the harm caused by the digital revolution. The digital revolution, as mentioned earlier, has many benefits for humanity but it has also created three major problems that as a global community we need to address. First, the digital revolution has allowed many technology companies to grow quickly economically but without sufficient regulation. Many of these companies fail to pay taxes and they fail to take responsibility when the technological service they have created has an undesirable effect on the common good of humanity. To respond to this first problem, the Republic Earth Organisation believes we need to rein in the unaccountable power of the digital revolution. Over the last 40 years, we have transferred power from governments into the hands of major corporations, including technology companies. It is time for power to return to a new form of democratic global governance of the digital revolution.

One of the big stories of 2016 was how so-called 'fake news' was able to spread on social media like Facebook during the 2016 US Presidential Election, with the result of affecting how people voted.[249] As a result, Facebook failed to quickly understand that there was a problem and only after interventions from government did it act to work on trying to fix the problem. The biggest issue with the 'fake news' issue is that now it is possible to use data to press our emotional buttons.

According to Yuval Harari, the digital bots 'might identify our deepest fears, hatreds, and cravings and use them against us. We have already been given a foretaste of this in recent elections and referendums across the world, when hackers learned how to manipulate individual voters by analysing data about them and exploiting their prejudices'.[250] This is just one example of a list of thousands where technology companies have felt there was no problem at all and were above the law but only after public pressure and interventions did they act to fix the problem. The Republic Earth Organisation believes we must do more to rein in the unaccountable power of the digital revolution and bring technology companies to account when they are not acting in the common good.

Second, the digital revolution is undermining the mental and physical health of millions of people around the world. Due to the rise in technology, we are experiencing an increase in depression, suicide (globally 800,000 committed suicide in 2012) and other mental health disorders among young people in particular, as well as an increase in addictions, such as to drugs, alcohol, pornography and gambling online.[251] We are also experiencing a decline in physical health as people fail to disconnect from the digital world and fail to undertake physical exercise on a weekly basis. Too many people in our digital world keep saying they are 'too busy' and, as a result, are failing to look after their mental or physical health.

Yuval Harari makes a valid point by saying that, 'Technology isn't bad. If you know what you want in life, technology can help you get it. But if you don't know what you want in life, it will be all too easy for technology to shape your aims for you and take control of your life. Especially as technology gets better at understanding humans, you might increasingly find yourself serving it, instead of it serving you. Have you seen those zombies who roam the streets with their faces glued to their smartphones? Do you think they control the technology, or does the technology control them?'[252] Now the worry is with the rise of virtual reality and artificial intelligence that people may see a further decline in their health, as they become addicted to other new forms of technology. The Republic Earth Organisation believes we must do all we can to improve people's health so that they enjoy the benefits of the digital revolution while not letting it undermine their mental and physical health.

Third, the control of the digital revolution is now starting to come into question, as technology companies seek to advance their interests and entities like the SCO seek to gain greater control of the digital revolution. The big game in town is controlling the data within the internet and through the digital revolution. The Republic Earth Organisation believes we should not only ensure technology companies do not have unfettered power but we should also not allow new entities like the

SCO to emerge and use sharp power, cyberterrorism and bullying to take control of the digital revolution.

Since 2014, China has held its own World Internet Conference, which promulgates the Chinese view of internet regulation. The digital revolution must remain a democratic institution where people's human rights and data are protected. The worry in the future is that a technology company or an entity like the SCO or an autocratic nation or third party will have control of all of the world's data free from regulation and could easily misuse it to the detriment of humanity. The Republic Earth Organisation wishes to encourage democratic countries to better regulate the digital revolution so that the world's data is protected.

On this point, Yuval Harari notes that, 'The biggest and most frightening impact of the AI revolution might be on the relative efficiency of democracies and dictatorships. Historically, autocracies have faced crippling handicaps in regard to innovation and economic growth. In the late 20th century, democracies usually outperformed dictatorships, because they were far better at processing information...However, artificial intelligence may soon swing the pendulum in the opposite direction. AI makes it possible to process enormous amounts of information centrally. In fact, it might make centralized systems far more efficient than diffuse systems, because machine learning works better when the machine has more information to analyse...Remember that the Internet, too, was hyped in its early days as a libertarian panacea that would free people from all centralized systems—but is now poised to make centralized authority more powerful than ever.'[253]

To avoid the pitfalls of the AI revolution, Yuval Harari suggests, 'if we want to prevent the concentration of all wealth and power in the hands of a small elite, we must regulate the ownership of data...In the 21st century, data will eclipse both land and machinery as the most important asset, so politics will be a struggle to control data's flow...The race to accumulate data is already on, and is currently headed by giants such as Google and Facebook and, in China, Baidu and Tencent...Nationalization of data by governments could offer one solution (to regulating the control of data); it would certainly curb the power of big corporations. But history suggests that we are not necessarily better off in the hands of overmighty governments. So we had better call upon our scientists, our philosophers, our lawyers, and even our poets to turn their attention to this big question: How do you regulate the ownership of data?' [254] This may well be one of the most important political questions of our era. If we cannot answer this question soon, our socio-political system might collapse.

The Republic Earth Organisation believes we cannot allow a digital dictatorship to emerge where a corporation or an entity like the SCO has access to all the world's data. We believe that democratic nations need to create a globally distributed data system where we collectively have access to the system and we collectively own the world's data. Thus, the world's data should not be centralised into any one company or nation state or an entity like the SCO.

The Republic Earth Organisation wants to create a global democracy, and by doing so we have a great chance to protect the world's data from being misused. Creating a globally distributed data system will be a great safeguard of democracy in the 21st century. We may need to create a new global data agency where democratic nations all share collective responsibility, and ordinary citizens, corporations and nations make requests to access data on an as-needs basis.

CHAPTER 21: THE THREAT POSED BY NUCLEAR WEAPONS

Another key global challenge to address is the threat of nuclear weapons. During the Cuban Missile Crisis of 1962, the world was extremely anxious about the outbreak of nuclear war between the US and Russia. Since 1962, nations possessing nuclear weapons have thankfully understood the consequences of their use and the possibility of triggering nuclear war, with devastating consequences for humanity.

According to the Stockholm International Peace Research Institute (SIPRI), nine nations hold a stockpile of approximately 14,935 nuclear warheads: USA, Russia, UK, France, China, India, Pakistan, Israel and North Korea.[255] Around 4,150 are believed to be operationally deployed.[256] According to the Federation of American Scientists, in 2018 nations having nuclear weapons included: Russia, 6,800 weapons; US, 6,600; France, 300; China, 270; UK, 215; Pakistan, 140; India, 13; Israel, 80; North Korea, 20.[257] This means that the SCO (China, Russia, Pakistan and North Korea) have 7,230 weapons; and democratic nations that hopefully will form part of the Republic Earth Organisation (USA, France, UK, India and Israel) have 7,325 weapons.

One of the great tragedies of the 21st century is that more nations are looking to acquire nuclear weapons. It has been deeply troubling that North Korea has emerged now to possess nuclear weapons as well. The Nuclear Nonproliferation Treaty allows only five states to have nuclear weapons, but there are now nine that do. The Republic Earth Organisation, led by Australia, hopes that no more nations seek to acquire nuclear weapons, such as Iran or Saudi Arabia. For the benefit of humanity and citizens around the world, we must do all we can to reduce stockpiles of nuclear weapons and prevent other nations from acquiring them.

One of the biggest threats nuclear weapons pose is that they could get into the hands of non-state actors or terrorist groups. This is why a Republic Earth Organisation is needed to create a new set of treaties to ensure we prevent more nations from acquiring them, as well as working to reduce current stockpiles and prevent non-state actors like terrorist groups from acquiring them. The last thing we want is a cash-strapped or vengeful North Korea selling one of its warheads for the right price. A more recent emerging threat is that a rogue group could hack into a nuclear power's command and control computers, triggering a launch, or into an early warning system, giving the impression an enemy attack is imminent.[258]

In Australia, it was pleasing that back in 2007 the International Campaign to Abolish Nuclear Weapons (ICAN) was founded in Melbourne to create a global civil society coalition to promote adherence to and full implementation of the Treaty on the Prohibition of Nuclear Weapons.[259] As a result of ICAN's efforts, in 2017 an Australian-led organisation in ICAN was awarded the Noble Peace Prize for its work of drawing attention to the catastrophic humanitarian consequences of any use of nuclear weapons and for its ground-breaking efforts to achieve a treaty-based prohibition of such weapons.[260] It is understood that such efforts do not necessarily reduce the risk that nuclear weapons still pose to humanity, but the work of ICAN has to be admired. Such global campaigns are what is needed to tackle one of the key challenges we face in the World of Disorder—the threat posed by nuclear weapons.

Despite the efforts of ICAN, Donald Trump has said the time may have come for the US to pull out of the Intermediate-Range Nuclear Forces Treaty (INF Treaty), which had been in force for over 30 years and was signed by US President Ronald Reagan and USSR's Mikhail Gorbachev.[261] According to Sean Fleming, 'The treaty was designed to limit the two countries' capacity to strike each other directly with land based missiles—those with a range of 500 to 5,500 kilometres. Since its implementation, the INF Treaty has led to the elimination of 2,692 missiles.'[262]

In light of Donald Trump's decision to withdraw from the INF Treaty with Russia in 2018, we may see a proliferation in the creation of nuclear weapons in countries such as the US, China and Russia. If this occurs, then Donald Trump has only increased the threat of nuclear weapons in the 21st century.

Donald Trump has also done nothing to undermine the threat of nuclear weapons posed by North Korea. On 12 June 2018, Donald Trump met with Kim Jong-un in Singapore; however, since the summit the threat has not been diminished, as the goal was to achieve a complete denuclearisation of the Korean peninsula.[263] Instead, in December 2018, North Korea stated that it will never unilaterally give up its nuclear weapons unless the US first removes what Pyongyang called a nuclear threat.[264] This statement suggests North Korea will eventually demand the US withdraw or significantly reduce the 28,500 American troops stationed in South Korea; a major sticking point in the disarmament deal.[265]

According to Kim Tong-Hyung, 'North Korea for decades has been pushing a concept of denuclearization that bears no resemblance to the American definition, with Pyongyang vowing to pursue nuclear development until the United States removes its troops and nuclear umbrella defending South Korea and Japan ... North Korea's reiteration of its long standing position on denuclearization could prove to be a major setback for diplomacy, which was revived early this year following a series of provocative nuclear and missile tests that left Kim and Trump spending most of 2017 exchanging personal insults and war threats.'[266] The key point to make is that the nuclear negotiations between Washington and Pyongyang have stalled since the Trump-Kim meeting and, if anything, the threat has increased and not decreased.

Over recent years we have witnessed a worsening of relations between nuclear armed states. With Russia and China building up its military forces as part of an SCO campaign, it is vital that democratic nations unite to reduce the threat posed by nuclear weapons. Nuclear risk reduction is a common security interest of all states—one that transcends alliances and umbrellas, and even the geopolitical circumstances that have stagnated arms control and disarmament. From a peak of 70,000 nuclear weapons in the world at the height of the Cold War in 1985, there are now about 14,000, according to the Federation of American Scientists.[267]

The threat from nuclear weapons will not be reduced until we unite all nations around a common global security agenda, and that is what the Republic Earth Organisation is committed to achieve in the 21st century.

CHAPTER 22: AUTOCRATIC REGIMES THREATENING DEMOCRATIC NATIONS

One global challenge we need to address is that of autocratic regimes threatening democratic nations. In the 20th century we had a battle between capitalism and communism that fuelled the Cold War, while between 1989 and 2001 we had a period of democratic supremacy. However, since the creation of the SCO in 2001, we have witnessed a rising form of authoritarian influence in the democratic world by its leading member nations China and Russia.

According to the National Endowment for Democracy Report, 'Over the past decade, China and Russia have spent billions of dollars to shape public opinion and perceptions around the world, employing a diverse toolkit that includes thousands of people-to-people exchanges, wide-ranging cultural activities, education programs, and the development of media enterprises and information initiatives with global reach ... Contrary to some prevailing analysis, the attempt by Beijing and Moscow to wield influence through initiatives in the spheres of media, culture, think tanks, and academia is neither a "charm offensive" nor an effort to "win hearts and minds," the common frame of reference for "soft power" efforts. This authoritarian influence is not principally about attraction or even persuasion; instead, it centers on distraction and manipulation. These ambitious authoritarian regimes, which systematically suppress political pluralism and free expression at home, are increasingly seeking to apply similar principles internationally to secure their interests.

'We are in need of a new vocabulary for this phenomenon. What we have to date understood as authoritarian "soft power" is better categorized as "sharp power" that pierces, penetrates, or perforates the political and information environments in the target countries. In this new competition that is under way between autocratic and democratic states, the repressive regimes' "sharp power" techniques should be seen as the tip of their dagger—or indeed as their syringe.'[268]

This chapter aims to unmask this form of sharp power and authoritarian influence used by China and Russia. We need to create new policies to inoculate democratic nations against malign authoritarian influence, reaffirm support for democratic values and ideals, and promote the idea of building a democratic global society or Republic Earth; and create a counter-revolution against sharp power and play hardball against this rising form of authoritarian influence around the world.

Since 2001, the SCO have not sought to use soft power to unite the world under their agenda because their autocratic agenda is not globally acceptable. Instead, China and Russia have sought to use sharp power and act as global bullies to take advantage of the openness of democratic societies like the US and Australia. Both China and Russia leverage a broad range of party, state and non-state actors to advance its influence-seeking objectives. Both seek to use sharp power to influence the political systems in countries around the world, on university campuses (for example, China currently has 512 Confucius institutes and 1,113 classrooms in over 146 countries around the world), at think tanks, in businesses, in media outlets, in technological and military sectors, and among both Chinese and Russian communities around the world.[269]

In many ways, China and Russia have a coordinated plan to use sharp power to steal power from democratic nations, so that autocratic and authoritarian nations can reign supreme in the 21st century. Democratic nations need to fight back by using sunshine to show what is going on. Sunshine is the best disinfectant against the manipulation of democratic entities by outside actors using foreign influence to seize power, and we should shine as much light as possible on Chinese and Russian influence-seeking over nations, organisations and individuals if it is covert, coercive or corrupting. Defending the integrity of democratic institutions requires standing up for our principles of openness and freedom, more closely coordinating responses within institutional sectors, and also better informing both governmental and nongovernmental actors about the potentially harmful influence activities of China and Russia and other foreign actors.

Both countries have heavily targeted the US to undermine their democracy, most recently during the 2016 US Presidential Election. In terms of media, both China and Russia have sought to get their CCTV and Russia Today networks into American hotels.[270] Moreover, both China and Russia are seeking to use soft power within media networks to complement their growing economic and military strengths. For example, in the US, China 'has established a radio network and a television network, which distribute state-controlled programming to American audiences. China also publishes newspapers and magazines here in Chinese and English, Chinese websites are available to Americans online, and the US readily gives work visas to Chinese reporters, who then feed content back to state-run propaganda organs at home. By contrast, American media aren't permitted to operate any television or radio networks in China, and the government partially or completely blocks the websites of most major US news organisations. The only American publications generally available focus on such topics as lifestyle and business, including Vogue, Elle, and special "China editions" of Forbes and the Harvard Business Review. The Chinese government also systematically blocks access to Twitter, Facebook, YouTube and Google'.[271]

Most notably in terms of politics, the US Office of the Director of National Intelligence stated that the Russian Government favoured presidential candidate Trump over Clinton, and that Russian President Vladimir Putin personally ordered an 'influence campaign' to harm Clinton's chances and 'undermine public faith in the US democratic process'.[272] The US continues to suffer cyberattacks, as mentioned previously, and not only has China sought to steal information from the US military but Chinese spies also undertook an attack with a tiny chip that reached almost 30 US companies, including Amazon and Apple, compromising America's technology supply chain.[273] This form of sharp power by both China and Russia is just a small snapshot of what has taken place since 2001 but still continues and is getting worse. The US has now woken up to the foreign influence, and how the Trump Administration responds will be interesting, as at present all they are doing is ceding the US's global power to China and Russia. In many ways, Donald Trump could be a so-called 'Manchurian Candidate', as much as a US President.

In Australia, Chinese influence has proceeded much further than it has in the US. From politics to culture, real estate to agriculture, universities to unions and even primary schools, there is compelling evidence of the Chinese Communist Party's infiltration of Australia. According to Clive Hamilton, 'Sophisticated influence operations target Australian elites, and parts of the large Chinese Australian diaspora have been mobilised to buy access to politicians, limit academic freedom, intimidate critics, collect information for Chinese intelligence agencies, and protest in the streets against Australian Government policies ... In 2016 it was revealed that wealthy Chinese businessmen linked to the Chinese Communist Party have become the largest donors to both major parties.'[274]

In one example, Chinese billionaire businessman Huang Xiangmo made donations to the Australian Labor Party and even encouraged former Labor Senator Sam Dastyari to contradict and condemn his own party's views on the South China Sea, stating that 'the Chinese integrity of its borders is a matter for China'.[275] In this case, Chinese sharp power through political donations was having the effect of potentially changing the foreign policy of the Australian Labor Party. Moreover, in October 2018, the Victorian State Labor Government signed onto China's Belt and Road Initiative via a comprehensive and elaborate sharp power technique of Chinese foreign influence.[276]

Meanwhile, according to Clive Hamilton, 'In May 2016 without any much fanfare, a high ranking Communist Party leader arrived in Australia. Liu Qibao heads the Chinese Communist Party Central Committee Propaganda Department ... in a development that seasoned journalists still find hard to fathom, Liu was in Australia to sign six agreements with the major Australian media outlets ... in exchange for money they would publish Chinese propaganda by outlets like Xinhua News Agency, the *People's Daily* and *China Daily* ... *The Sydney Morning Herald*, *The Age* and the *Australian Financial Review* agreed to carry monthly eight page lift outs supplied by *China Daily*.'[277]

In Australia, the Chinese-owned State Grid Corporation owns parts of our energy network including three of Victoria's five electricity distributors and the transmitting network in South Australia.[278] A 99-year lease of Darwin Port was sold to a Chinese company with close links to the CCP in 2015.[279] This was in part because of the work of former Liberal Trade Minister Andrew Robb, who stepped directly from office into a consultancy job with a CCP company that bought Darwin Port.[280] We have also witnessed Huawei wishing to obtain the lucrative 5G contract to gain a further sharp power advantage in Australia's telecommunications network, but now Huawei has been denied by the Australian Government.[281]

According to Clive Hamilton, 'In 2013 *Four Corners* reported that the most important government departments had been penetrated by China-based hackers, including the prime minister's department, the defence department, foreign affairs and the Australian Overseas Intelligence Agency, the Australian Secret Intelligence Service.'[282] In 2019, the Australian Parliament House Computer Network and the computer networks of the three main political parties were hacked by a 'sophisticated state actor', most likely China.[283] The extent of foreign influence led the director general of the Australian Security Intelligence Organisation, Duncan Lewis, to say that espionage and the foreign influence threat is greater now than at any time during the Cold War.[284]

In light of this growing form of foreign influence, Australia in 2018 created a new counter-foreign-interference strategy and has also introduced bipartisan legislation into the Australian parliament. The Foreign Influence Transparency Scheme Bill 2018 requires registration of individuals or entities undertaking activities on behalf of 'foreign principals'.[285] The amended Espionage and Foreign Interference Bill was also introduced to create new spying offences, update sabotage offences and a new offence relating to the theft of trade secrets on behalf of a foreign government.[286] Another bill introduced a wide-reaching ban on foreign donations, while work was being done to better protect Australia's critical infrastructure from being affected by foreign influence.[287]

Randall Schriver, the Pentagon's senior official for Asia, said Australia has 'woken up people in a lot of countries to take a look at Chinese activity within their own borders'.[288] Hillary Clinton, the former US Presidential Candidate, said Australia has sounded the alarm on 'a new global battle'.[289] In many ways Australia is the leading nation in tackling this key challenge of autocratic regimes threatening democratic nations.

In Canada in 2010, the director of Canada's national security agency said that at least two provincial cabinet members and other governmental officials were under the control of foreign countries, including China.[290] In 2016, Prime Minister Justin Trudeau was the subject of controversy for his attendance at cash-for-access dinners.[291] Among the attendees were Chinese billionaire Zhang Bin, who donated $1 million to the Pierre Elliot Trudeau Foundation.[292]

In December 2017, the *Globe and Mail* reported that two Conservative senators had set up a private consulting business with the intent of attracting Chinese investment to Newfoundland and Labrador.[293] In response to growing foreign influence and a breach of US sanctions, Canada arrested one of the vice chairs on Huawei's board, Meng Wangzhou, in December 2018. She was later released but in response China detained 13 Canadian citizens after the arrest.[294] It appears China is not happy that its foreign influence operations are being exposed and key people are being arrested, so it decided to detain Canadian citizens unnecessarily, which infringed their human rights and civil liberties.

In the UK, both China and Russia have made a concerted effort to use sharp power to gain influence; for example, Russia interfering in the 2016 Brexit Referendum, which has destabilised the country ever since.[295] The Chinese have recently struck deals worth $70 billion in the UK alone.[296] Both China and Russia have focused on buying up London's commercial real estate, and Chinese firms are involved in strategic parts of the British economy, including telecommunications and nuclear power.[297] *China Daily* now distributes its China Watch supplement as an advertisement inside the respected conservative newspaper *The Daily Telegraph*.[298] For years Chinese telecom behemoth Huawei has provided broadband gear and mobile networks to its clients in Britain.[299]

Another area of growing concern is nuclear power. China General Nuclear Power (GNP)—the main player in China's nuclear industry—is considering the purchase of a 49 per cent stake in the UK's existing nuclear plants.[300] Meanwhile, on 4 March 2018, Sergei Skripal (a former Russian military officer and double agent for the UK's intelligence services), and his daughter Yulia Skripal, were poisoned in Salisbury, England, with a Novichok nerve agent that was supposedly carried out by Russian

FSB Agents.[301] The problem with the UK currently is that with Brexit consuming all the political oxygen, they have failed to properly combat this growing form of foreign influence on their shores.

In Argentina over the last five years, China has established a presence in almost every sphere of life. Politically, ties between Buenos Aires and Beijing are experiencing a golden age, even after elections at the end of 2015 swung power from one end of the political spectrum to the other.[302] Beijing has already provided $20 billion in loans to finance a handful of large-scale infrastructure projects.[303] Grupo America, Argentina's second-largest media corporation, closed an agreement with *China Daily* to insert the four-page China Watch supplement twice a month in five of the group's newspapers, including *El Cronista*, the country's top business daily.[304] While in October 2014, just three months after Putin's visit to Argentina, *Russia Today en Espanol* began to broadcast on Argentina's public television platform, which meant an audience of around 35 million people could potentially access the Russian Channel for free 24 hours a day.[305] Both China and Russia have exerted foreign influence in every country in Latin America.

From Africa to Asia, the Chinese and Russian sharp power is fully entrenched. In Djibouti in September 2017, China built its first overseas military base at Doraleh.[306] In Zimbabwe, Russia has been cultivating economic ties, including a $3 billion investment in platinum mining, while also pursuing deeper military ties.[307] In Sri Lanka the government handed over control of the Hambantota Port to China.[308] While Russia dispatched autocratic election monitors to Cambodia to ensure Hun Sen's Cambodian People's Party won 125 of 125 seats.[309] No matter what country in the world, both China and Russia are using sharp power to gain greater power.

In particular, according to Oriana Skylar Mastro, 'Beijing has been especially innovative in its use of economic power. The strategy here has been to finance infrastructure in the developing world in order to create dependent, and thus compliant, foreign governments. Most recently, those efforts have taken the form of the Belt and Road Initiative, a massive regional infrastructure project launched in 2013. China has spent about $400 billion on the initiative (and pledged hundreds of billions of dollars more), and it has convinced 86 countries and international organizations to sign some 100 related cooperation agreements. Chinese aid, which primarily takes the form of loans from banks controlled by the Chinese Communist Party, doesn't come with the usual Western strings attached: there are no requirements for market reforms or better governance. What China does demand from recipients, however, is allegiance on a number of issues, including the nonrecognition of Taiwan.'[310]

In nearly every country in the world, the SCO leading member nations of China and Russia are using sharp power to grow their power and take power away from democratic nations. For example, at the start of 2019, Chinese President Xi Jinping made it clear that Taiwan's reunification with China is inevitable. While Russia was firmly committed to interfere in the Ukraine Presidential Election in March 2019 to help elect a pro-Russian regime. Both China and Russia wish to expand their empires and spheres of influence to ensure that Taiwan becomes part of China and the Ukraine becomes a Russian proxy state. Democratic nations need to support the citizens in both Taiwan and Ukraine. If the people of these nations want to support the autocratic views of China and Russia through the SCO, then we need to accept that decision. However, many people in Taiwan and Ukraine support democracy, the rule of law and the protection of human rights, and would not want to see their countries slide into the autocratic world.

The Republic Earth Organisation believes that a two-thirds vote by people in Taiwan and Ukraine would need to agree to any transition to the autocratic world. It is an important and long-lasting decision for a nation, and when both are democratic there should be a higher bar set on a vote if democracy is going to cease to exist in their countries. Nations like Australia should do all we can to promote and protect democracy around the world.

In 2019 and 2020 there are a number of notable democratic elections occurring around the world, and the worry is that both China and Russia, through the SCO, will seek to use cyberterrorism, fake news or even AI to interfere in these elections so as to undermine the principle of democracy. We must do all we can over the next two years to reduce the threat posed by these autocratic regimes, which seek to weaken and undermine democracy.

One thing to point out is that there is nothing inevitable about democracy, especially with the rising autocratic and authoritarian foreign influence of China and Russia around the world. According to Yuval Harari, 'for all the success that democracies have had over the past century or more, they are blips in history. Monarchies, oligarchies, and other forms of authoritarian rule have been far more common modes of human governance'.[311]

In light of this, the Republic Earth Organisation is fully committed to protecting democracy in the 21st century. We are also committed to creating new policies to inoculate democratic nations against malign authoritarian influence. The new pieces of legislation introduced in Australia in 2018 are a good first step for nations to look at when countering foreign influence in their countries.

The Republic Earth Organisation also wants democratic nations to unite to deal with the global concerted effort by the SCO and its leading member nations China and Russia to undermine democracy, by creating a new global entity like a Republic Earth Organisation to play hardball against this rising authoritarian influence. We also want to promote democratic ideals globally and raise awareness of the democratic fight we are in against authoritarianism.

The Republic Earth Organisation wants the world and the citizens of the world to reaffirm support for democratic values and ideals and promote the idea of building a democratic global society or democratic Republic Earth. This will be the only way we can truly counter this key challenge of the 21st century.

CONCLUSION

Ω

This book has attempted to help make sense of the current challenges democratic nations face, and is using a new political idea of a Republic Earth to help unite the world in the 21st century and build a successful global society. According to Bret Stephens, the Liberal Democratic World or the West is currently 'rudderless' in light of Brexit and the US Trump Presidency, and the goal of this book is to argue that the idea of a Republic Earth could help to give the Liberal Democratic World a sense of direction once more.[312]

It is exciting to work on ideas that aim to unite the world, just as music or a sporting event can; however, as the world increasingly becomes more interconnected, we are facing a choice. Do we want an autocratic worldview or a democratic worldview to build the World of Order and the global society, and deal with the World of Disorder and the key challenges facing humanity in the 21st century? Former US President Roosevelt, in the latter stages of World War II, worked on building a democratic global society and established the United Nations to try to unite the world for the common good. The UN was designed to build global society in the 20th century and deal with the key global security threats. The UN has done an amazing amount of work over the last 74 years to create a more united world and generations of people have enjoyed a better quality of life. However, the UN needs reform, and with autocratic nations growing in influence it is unlikely to be able to keep the world united.

In 2001, the Shanghai Cooperation Organization emerged without much notice amongst democratic nations. Most thought it was a new international organisation similar to APEC or ASEAN, but it is clear the SCO is designed to undo the work of the UN and instead build an autocratic, authoritarian and potentially fascist global society in the 21st century. It is quite clear to see a future where the so-called Global Capital moves from New York to Shanghai and the SCO replaces the UN. Within 15 years this reality could occur and the SCO could unite the world under a different agenda, and thus democratic nations have a choice. Do we work within the UN to reform it and make it better to counter autocratic foreign influence and the rise of the SCO? This will be difficult as both China and Russia are permanent members of the UN Security Council and will veto such an action. Or do democratic nations build a new global democratic organisation, like a Republic Earth Organisation, to counter the threat posed by the SCO?

This book argues that only by creating a new global democratic organisation can we protect democracy, build a global democracy, build a global society, and address the key challenges facing humanity today. Whether we like it or not, we are now in the midst of a major global battle between democracy and autocracy as the best model for uniting the world. This is one of the most important political questions of our age.

Democracy does need a reboot, but that is how the idea of a Republic Earth can help to excite the world to a more positive future, otherwise the rise of sharp power and bullying behaviour used by Chinese and Russian governments could undermine our current and growing World of Order and lead to a World of Disorder we cannot get out of and potentially threaten the existence of humanity itself. Perhaps Republic Earth is not the answer; however, something has to be done by democratic nations to stop us slipping into an authoritarian global world controlled by China and Russia where everyone is monitored, like in an Orwellian state, and the freedoms people take for granted right now will no longer exist.

This book hopes that democratic nations can unite to fight back and work out a plan to counter the autocratic threat posed by the SCO. Republic Earth could provide the solution and also provide a new hope, not only for Australia but for the world; and the formal creation of a Republic Earth Organisation could help to unite the world and render the SCO redundant. We argue that the SCO should never had been created and any grievance China and Russia had should have been brought to the United Nations. At no time have China and Russia expressed any major concerns, nor have they proposed reforms to the UN. Instead, they created the SCO to seize global power for themselves, and now democratic nations must play hardball and fight back.

It is important to note that Chinese President Xi Jinping is 65 years old and Russian President Vladimir Putin is 66 years old, so over the next 15 years, if both their rules remain unchallenged, they will seek to gain power over the world by 2034 in an autocratic manner. Hence, we need to create a counter-revolution against autocracy, authoritarianism and fascism, and ensure that democracy is not only rebooted and reformed, but reigns supreme in the 21st century to ensure the growing World of Order is protected and the democratic global society or Republic Earth succeeds.

CHAPTER 23: WORLD OF DISORDER CONCLUSION

i The Rise of the Shanghai Cooperation Organization

It is difficult to predict the future, but one possible outcome is that the SCO and its leading member nations, China and Russia, achieve their goal by 2030 by using sharp power to successfully unite most nations behind an autocratic and authoritarian agenda. One may argue that an autocratic World of Order may be preferable, but when democracy has been one of humanity's greatest achievements, as it has been able to govern the complex society of people in most nations around the world, it would be devastating to lose democracy in the 21st century. An auto-cratic society will mean Chinese and Russian companies will reign su-preme, and people living in countries like Australia will be pressured into utilising the goods and services from companies such as Huawei, Alibaba, Tencent, Ant Financial, Baidu, etc.

It is likely that an autocratic Orwellian global nation state would be created where the world's data is in the hands of the SCO and everyone would be constantly monitored to supress any dissent. Militarily, eco-nomically, culturally and socially, the SCO will control every part of a person's life and it will be difficult for democratic dissent to emerge because it will quickly be suppressed. We are not saying that China and Russia cannot gain greater power in the 21st century, but that their au-tocratic worldview is not in tune with the current views of the global society. If we want to protect the current global society we enjoy at present, we need to ensure that the SCO, and therefore China and Rus-sia, do not seize global power in an autocratic manner in the next 15 years.

ii World of Disorder—Out of Control

One possible future in the next 15 years is that the seven key global challenges discussed earlier (climate change, inequality, terrorism and cyberterrorism, refugees, nuclear weapons and autocratic regimes threatening democratic nations) get out of control and new challenges are added to this list. If over the next 15 years every key global challenge gets significantly worse, then humanity's existence will come into question. There is a very real risk that the World of Disorder will get out of control, or that it will be increasingly difficult to fully counter threats like climate change. The SCO has yet to commit solutions to all of these global challenges. Hence, it is up to democratic nations to unite and form a new global organisation that can fully address each of these challenges, so that this does not happen.

iii The SCO's Ambitions Lead to World War III

Another possible future in the next 15 years is that to gain global power the SCO goes to war against democratic states. Graham Allison notes that due to a Thucydides Trap, China and the US could be destined for war. Allison writes, 'Today, as an unstoppable China approaches an immovable America, and both Xi Jinping and Donald Trump promise to make their countries 'great again' ... Unless China is willing to scale back its ambitions or Washington can accept becoming number two in the Pacific, a trade conflict, cyberattack, or accident at sea could escalate into all-out war'.[313]

If China and Russia go to war against democratic nations, then a World War III would be a catastrophic event because it would come at a time when the seven key global challenges in the World of Disorder must be addressed. If such a war occurred, then issues like climate change would be even harder to solve. The Republic Earth Organisation sincerely hopes that the SCO and its leading nations China and Russia do not go to war to seize global power in an autocratic manner, as it will be a disaster for humanity and only significantly increase the World of Disorder in the 21st century.

CHAPTER 24: WORLD OF ORDER CONCLUSION

i Democratic Nations Check Rise of SCO

In terms of providing a possible future in the World of Order, we could see democratic nations unite in the coming years to check the rise of the autocratic SCO. China and Russia would likely remain autocratic states, but democratic nations would have united to prevent them using sharp power to gain global power. In many ways this would mean that Xi Jinping and Vladimir Putin would have failed in their quests to make autocratic regimes under their tenures triumph in the 21st century. Democratic nations may have set up a new democratic international organisation or rebooted the UN to succeed in their quest. The exposure of the autocratic worldview and the power of democracy would have convinced the citizens of the world that we needed to check the rise of the SCO, China and Russia. However, democratic nations would have yet to fully deal with the seven key global challenges in the World of Disorder.

ii Republic Earth Starts to Control the World of Disorder

One possible future is that the idea of a Republic Earth inspires democratic nations to create a Republic Earth Organisation, which not only curtails the rise of the SCO but also starts to address and get under control the seven key global challenges in the World of Disorder. In 2019, Australia could request to join the G7—the elite body of democratic nations—and by creating a G8 make the request for democratic nations to create a Republic Earth Organisation to meet the challenges posed by the SCO, and to address the increasing threats posed by the World of Disorder. One key success would be getting countries like India and Indonesia to be key members of the Republic Earth Organisation so as to curtail the power of China and Russia, and lessen the risk of them seizing global power in an autocratic manner.

iii Republic Earth Unites the World in the 21st Century

The final possible future suggested by this book is the idea that a Republic Earth could not only encourage democratic nations to unite to create a global democratic international organisation to build a new World of Order and address the World of Disorder, but it could help to unite the world in the 21st century. The Republic Earth idea could encourage people in China and Russia to demand the creation of a global democratic society and extinguish the threat posed by autocracy, authoritarianism or fascism. Over the next 15 years, Republic Earth could lead to China and Russia becoming full democracies, and thus the whole world would hopefully become democratic. As a result, China and Russia could build new and exciting democracies that inspire the world, meaning that the Republic Earth idea would actually make the people living within these countries enjoy a better quality of life. If the Republic Earth idea gains traction and we create a Republic Earth Organisation, then we have a great chance to not only build a successful new global democratic society and World of Order (where the global middle class expands, a global renewable energy economy is achieved, the digital revolution is accessible to everyone, gender equality and the wave of transparency flourish, medical breakthroughs flourish, new global governance structures are created, and a new political idea of Republic Earth inspires a new global way of thinking and celebrates the diversity of humanity), but also that Republic Earth and the creation of the Republic Earth Organisation can help to address the seven key global challenges of the 21st century.

The Republic Earth idea means that the US would need to abdicate from being a global superpower, and China would need to abdicate plans for being the global superpower, too, as the focus would be on ensuring the global society or the Republic Earth succeeds. No more American exceptionalism or Chinese exceptionalism—let's focus on the whole world and celebrate the greatness of humanity.

In 2019, Australia can begin the journey by calling for a Republic Earth Organisation to unite the world. A first step would be to create a Republic Earth Music Festival to unite the world through music on New Year's Eve. Back in 1939 Franklin Roosevelt began his journey of creating a

United Nations via hosting the 1939 New York Work Fair that showcased 'the world of tomorrow' from 33 participant countries, and had over 44 million people attend the fair. The Republic Earth Music Festival wishes to embody the same spirit to unite the world in the 2020s by uniting 206 nations each year on NYE via an online music democracy contest. The next step is to unite the world politically via democracy and through the establishment of a Republic Earth Organisation, which would work with the United Nations to unite the world in the 21st century. The United Nations should not cease to exist but a Republic Earth Organisation is needed to meet the autocratic challenge posed by the SCO. The Republic Earth Organisation should work together with the UN to achieve a more united world.

Australia has an opportunity to make our mark on the world stage. According to *The Economist*, Australia in 2018 'has been growing for 27 years without a recession—a record for a developed country. Its cumulative growth over that period is almost three times what Germany has managed. The median income has risen four times faster than in America. Public debt, at 41 per cent of GDP, is less than half Britain's ... Some 29 per cent of [Australia's] inhabitants were born in another country—twice the proportion in the United States. Half of Australians are either immigrants themselves or children of immigrants.'[314] In light of this success, Australia needs to make its mark on the world stage. The creation of a Republic Earth Organisation can be our great success story of the 21st century where we choose democracy and choose to unite the world. Hopefully in 2019 we can join the G7 group of leading democratic nations and create a G8. In 2020, hopefully we can convince the G8 to create a Republic Earth Organisation that aims to use the power of the idea to unite the world.

Republic Earth understands that in the 21st century we are in a great power competition between democracy and autocracy. According to Oriana Skylar Mastro and Jeane Kirkpatrick, 'The United States needs to recommit to protecting its values. Some in the Washington establishment speak longingly about Beijing's ability to get things done, thanks in part to its disregard for liberal norms. Indeed, this sort of agnosticism does give China an advantage. It is able to win over Asian governments by doling out money with no strings attached, its state-owned enterprises receive not just state support but also proprietary information through espionage, and its authoritarian political system makes it far easier to control the narrative about its goals and missions both at home and abroad. But China has an Achilles' heel: its leaders have failed to articulate a vision of global dominance that is beneficial for any country but China. That is why, unlike the United States, it prefers to work with weak partners that can be easily controlled. To be competitive, Washington cannot stoop to Beijing's level. The United States does not by any means have a perfect track record of living up to its values, but by and large, it has chosen to lead the world in a way that ensures that others also benefit. Now is not the time to abandon this inclusive approach. Washington should support the international institutions that make up the liberal order. It should dedicate greater resources to defending its allies and partners. And in its economic assistance, it should focus on quality over quantity, seeking to make sure that as many people as possible benefit from development. What has made the United States number one is that it thinks globally—not just about "America first". Only by expanding the reach of its own liberal values can the United States weather China's challenge.'[315]

Republic Earth believes the US and democratic nations like Australia can withstand this challenge posed by China and Russia and the SCO, but we must play hardball and use the idea of Republic Earth to put forward a better vision for the world.

Graham Allison states that, 'Support for economic integration is no longer a given, particularly as more and more people believe globalization has left them behind, fuelling a surge of populism, nationalism, and xenophobia ... [however] more elusive but unquestionably real is an emerging global consciousness among the planet's most active "golden billion" inhabitants. To a degree unseen in history, they have come to share perceptions, norms and practices. Ubiquitous communication networks have shrunk the globe, allowing elites everywhere to be aware of almost everything, and almost instantly. Smartphones bring images and words from every corner of the Earth. Explosions, hurricanes, and discoveries anywhere impact consciousness everywhere. The experience of international travel, not only by the global elite but also by average citizens, is now commonplace. Some 800,000 of China's best and brightest go abroad for their education, 300,000 studying in the US. Pause to think about the fact that the current President of China and his wife sent their only child to college not at Xi's alma mater of Tsinghua University, but rather at Harvard, where she graduated in 2014. How the views of an emerging generation of internationalists can be reconciled with the more nationalistic or populist inclinations of their fellow citizens is a puzzle. Finding ways in which the internationalists' understanding of the world can be translated into new forms of cooperation remains among the most intriguing opportunities.'[316] Hence, the idea of a Republic Earth is an opportunity to celebrate this golden generation of internationalists.

This book is trying to achieve four outcomes. First, to make sense of the 21st century, and show how the 20th century was a battle between capitalism and communism, whereas now we are in a battle between a World of Order and a World of Disorder.

Second, to celebrate the emergence of a new global society and a new World of Order. We argue that we need to continue to foster the development of the global society and create a democratic global organisation like the Republic Earth Organisation. This will continue to strengthen the development of the global society and the World of Order, and work on addressing the seven key global challenges.

Third, to encourage democratic nations to get back to the goal of uniting the world under a liberal, democratic, global agenda. Democratic nations have tried three times to unite the world under a global agenda. After World War I, democratic nations created the League of Nations but it failed. After World War II, democratic nations created the UN, which still exists and plays a major role in solving global issues; however, after 74 years the world has yet to become fully united under a liberal, democratic, global agenda. After the Cold War, the G7 emerged as the preeminent body to lead the democratic agenda, but since 2001 it has become distracted and lost its focus on uniting the world. Accordingly, by creating a Republic Earth Organisation we can work in partnership with the UN to finally succeed in a fourth attempt to achieve the goal of uniting the world under a liberal, democratic, global agenda.

Conclusion

Finally, this book wishes to enlighten Australians and all citizens around the world that since 2001 autocratic regimes through the SCO, led by co-founders China and Russia, have been on a coordinated campaign to use sharp power to weaken and take power away from democratic nations in a sophisticated way. In 2019, the SCO has used these tactics in all nations around the world. Without playing hardball and fighting back, autocratic nations could, within the next 10 to 15 years, gain global power and potentially unite the world under an autocratic and potentially fascist global agenda. In light of this reality, democratic nations led by the G7 need to unite and create a new global organisation to counter this threat and expose the autocratic worldview, and hopefully unite the world behind a brand-new liberal, democratic, Republic Earth global agenda.

In the 21st century, it is vital that we create a new global organisation. It does not need to be called the Republic Earth Organisation and does not need to be led by Australia, but a democratic nation or a group of nations need to reform the G7 to counter the threat posed by the autocratic SCO, and to ensure we foster continual growth and celebrate the emergence of the global society where more and more young people not only see themselves as citizens of a nation but as global citizens as well. This global society does not want to endure an autocratic social credit system that monitors their every move; they want to continue to live in an open, democratic society. Hence, through the Republic Earth project and creating a Republic Earth Organisation, we will work continuously to protect the principle of democracy, and fight to build a global democratic society that finally unites the world.

CHAPTER 25: FINAL POINT

In 2019 Larry Diamond (Senior Fellow at the Freeman Spogli Institute for International Studies - Democracy Expert from Stanford University) will explain this key issue of our age of autocratic nations threatening democratic nations in his 2019 book entitled *Ill Winds: Saving Democracy from Russian Rage, Chinese Ambition, and American Complacency.* This book aims to provide the solution to the challenge facing democratic nations from autocratic nations by creating a Republic Earth Organisation to replace the G7 in the 21st century to create a Global Democracy.

CHAPTER 26: GLOBAL ELECTION

Whether people like it or not global citizens and nation states will now have to start to decide do they prefer an autocratic or democratic global agenda. It is a clear choice and this book hopes people choose the democratic global agenda for the 21st century.

- See Appendix I—Letter from Franklin D. Roosevelt to Adolf Hitler, dated 14 April 1939.

- See Appendix II—Letter to Xi Jinping, dated 1 October 2019.

APPENDIX I

14th April 1939[317]

His Excellency Adolf Hitler,
Chancellor of the German Reich,
Berlin, Germany

You realize, I am sure, that throughout the world hundreds of millions of human beings are living today in constant fear of a new war or even a series of wars.

The existence of this fear—and the possibility of such a conflict—are of definite concern to the people of the United States for whom I speak, as they must also be to the peoples of the other nations of the entire Western Hemisphere. All of them know that any major war, even if it were to be confined to other continents, must bear heavily on them during its continuance and also for generations to come.

Because of the fact that after the acute tension in which the world has been living during the past few weeks there would seem to be at least a momentary relaxation—because no troops are at this moment on the march—this may be an opportune moment for me to send you this message.

On a previous occasion I have addressed you in behalf of the settlement of political, economic, and social problems by peaceful methods and without resort to arms.

But the tide of events seems to have reverted to the threat of arms. If such threats continue, it seems inevitable that much of the world must become involved in common ruin. All the world, victor nations, vanquished nations, and neutral nations, will suffer. I refuse to believe that the world is, of necessity, such a prisoner of destiny. On the contrary, it is clear that the leaders of great nations have it in their power to liberate their peoples from the disaster that impends. It is equally clear that in their own minds and in their own hearts the peoples themselves desire that their fears be ended.

It is, however, unfortunately necessary to take cognizance of recent facts.

Three nations in Europe and one in Africa have seen their independent existence terminated. A vast territory in another independent Nation of the Far East has been occupied by a neighboring State. Reports, which we trust are not true, insist that further acts of aggression are contemplated against still other independent nations. Plainly the world is moving toward the moment when this situation must end in catastrophe unless a more rational way of guiding events is found. You have repeatedly asserted that you and the German people have no desire for war. If this is true there need be no war.

Nothing can persuade the peoples of the earth that any governing power has any right or need to inflict the consequences of war on its own or any other people save in the cause of self-evident home defense.

In making this statement we as Americans speak not through selfishness or fear or weakness. If we speak now it is with the voice of strength and with friendship for mankind. It is still clear to me that international problems can be solved at the council table.

It is therefore no answer to the plea for peaceful discussion for one side to plead that unless they receive assurances beforehand that the verdict will be theirs, they will not lay aside their arms. In conference rooms, as in courts, it is necessary that both sides enter upon the discussion in good faith, assuming that substantial justice will accrue to both; and it is customary and necessary that they leave their arms outside the room where they confer.

I am convinced that the cause of world peace would be greatly advanced if the nations of the world were to obtain a frank statement relating to the present and future policy of Governments.

Because the United States, as one of the Nations of the Western Hemisphere, is not involved in the immediate controversies which have arisen in Europe, I trust that you may be willing to make such a statement of policy to me as head of a Nation far removed from Europe in order that I, acting only with the responsibility and obligation of a friendly intermediary, may communicate such declaration to other nations now apprehensive as to the course which the policy of your Government may take.

Are you willing to give assurance that your armed forces will not attack or invade the territory or possessions of the following independent nations: Finland, Estonia, Latvia, Lithuania, Sweden, Norway, Denmark, The Netherlands, Belgium, Great Britain and Ireland, France, Portugal, Spain, Switzerland, Liechtenstein, Luxembourg, Poland, Hungary, Rumania, Yugoslavia, Russia, Bulgaria, Greece, Turkey, Iraq, the Arabias, Syria, Palestine, Egypt and Iran?

Such an assurance clearly must apply not only to the present day but also to a future sufficiently long to give every opportunity to work by peaceful methods for a more permanent peace. I therefore suggest that you construe the word "future" to apply to a minimum period of assured non-aggression—ten years at the least—a quarter of a century, if we dare look that far ahead.

If such assurance is given by your Government, I shall immediately transmit it to the Governments of the nations I have named and I shall simultaneously inquire whether, as I am reasonably sure, each of the nations enumerated will in turn give like assurance for transmission to you.

Reciprocal assurances such as I have outlined will bring to the world an immediate measure of relief.

I propose that if it is given, two essential problems shall promptly be discussed in the resulting peaceful surroundings, and in those discussions the Government of the United States will gladly take part.

The discussions which I have in mind relate to the most effective and immediate manner through which the peoples of the world can obtain progressive relief from the crushing burden of armament which is each day bringing them more closely to the brink of economic disaster. Simultaneously the Government of the United States would be prepared to take part in discussions looking toward the most practical manner of opening up avenues of international trade to the end that every Nation of the earth may be enabled to buy and sell on equal terms in the world market as well as to possess assurance of obtaining the materials and products of peaceful economic life.

At the same time, those Governments other than the United States which are directly interested could undertake such political discussions as they may consider necessary or desirable.

We recognize complex world problems which affect all humanity but we know that study and discussion of them must be held in an atmosphere of peace. Such an atmosphere of peace cannot exist if negotiations are overshadowed by the threat of force or by the fear of war.

I think you will not misunderstand the spirit of frankness in which I send you this message. Heads of great Governments in this hour are literally responsible for the fate of humanity in the coming years. They cannot fail to hear the prayers of their peoples to be protected from the fore-seeable chaos of war. History will hold them accountable for the lives and the happiness of all—even unto the least.

I hope that your answer will make it possible for humanity to lose fear and regain security for many years to come.

A similar message is being addressed to the Chief of the Italian Government.

Franklin D. Roosevelt
32nd President of the United States of America

APPENDIX II

1st October 2019

Xi Jinping
President of the People's Republic of China,
Beijing, China.

You realize, I am sure, that throughout the world we are dealing with increasing threats to humanity in the 21st century, with millions of human beings being affected and the world needing to take action on climate change, inequality, terrorism and cyberterrorism, displaced peoples and refugees, harm caused by the digital revolution, threat posed by nuclear weapons, and autocratic regimes threatening democratic nations.

We are requesting that the People's Republic of China join member states of the United Nations in fully addressing each of these seven key global challenges facing humanity.

The global community, in particular democratic nations, are extremely concerned that since 2001, through the Shanghai Cooperation Organization, both China and Russia, as the leading states of the SCO, are using a form of sharp power to threaten democratic nations rather than fully addressing each of the urgent seven key global challenges facing humanity.

The Republic Earth Organisation was created in Australia in September 2014, and we were delighted to hear that when you visited Australia in November 2014 you had the goal of China becoming a full democracy by 2050. In light of the threat posed by sharp power towards democratic nations, we urge China and Russia to end its use of this sharp power and both commit to become full democracies by 2020, not 2050. In the first half of the 20th century, Chinese and Australians fought together in two world wars and jointly upheld world peace and human justice. In 1972, China and Australia entered into diplomatic ties, which opened a new chapter of friendship and cooperation in the relations between our two countries. Unless China commits to democracy by 2020, we believe the democratic Republic Earth Organisation will need to challenge the sharp power threat being posed by the autocratic SCO.

One nation in Europe, namely Ukraine, and one nation in Asia, namely Taiwan (Republic of China), are seeing their independent existence threatened. Reports, which we trust are not true, insist that further acts of aggression are contemplated against still other independent nations. Plainly, the world in the coming years is moving toward the moment when this situation must end in catastrophe unless a more rational way of guiding events is found. You have repeatedly asserted that you and the Chinese people have no desire for war. If this is true, there need be no war.

Nothing can persuade the peoples of the Earth that any governing power has any right or need to inflict the consequences of war on its own or any other people save in the cause of self-evident home defence.

In making this statement, the Republic Earth Organisation speaks not through selfishness or fear or weakness. If we speak now it is with the voice of strength and with friendship for mankind. It is still clear to me that international problems can be solved through the UN Security Council.

I am convinced that the cause of world peace would be greatly advanced if the nations of the world were to obtain a frank statement relating to the present and future policies of the Chinese Government.

Are you willing to give assurance that your armed forces will not attack or invade the territory or possessions of the following independent nations: Taiwan (Republic of China), Philippines, Vietnam, Malaysia, Japan, Sri Lanka, Indonesia, Pakistan, India, Ukraine, Australia or any other nation in the world?

Such an assurance clearly must apply not only to the present day but also to a future sufficiently long to give every opportunity to work by peaceful methods for a more permanent peace. I therefore suggest that you construe the word 'future' to apply to a minimum period of assured non-aggression—ten years at the least—a quarter of a century, if we dare look that far ahead.

If such assurance is given by your Government, I shall immediately transmit it to the governments of the nations I have named.

Reciprocal assurances such as I have outlined will bring to the world an immediate measure of relief.

We recognise complex world problems that affect all humanity, but we know that study and discussion of them must be held in an atmosphere of peace. Such an atmosphere of peace cannot exist if negotiations are overshadowed by the continued use of sharp power by the SCO. We are also deeply concern by the Chinese Government's treatment of Uighurs in Xinjiang Provence; and the people living in Hong Kong who are pro-testing and demanding democracy for Hong Kong. People around the world are calling for more democracy not less and it would be great for China to work with democratic nations like Australia to create a Global Democracy.

I hope that your answer will make it possible for humanity to lose fear and regain security for many years to come.

We urge you as President of the People's Republic of China to outline China's ambition for the 21st century and be fully transparent post the celebrations of the 70th Anniversary of the People's Republic of China on 1 October 2019. China should work with democratic nations to sort out any concerns and work in partnership with the United Nations to create a united world.

A similar message is being addressed to the President of the Russian Federation.

Daniel White
Citizen of Australia (Global Citizen)
Founder of the Republic Earth Organisation

ENDNOTES

1   Avneet Aroram 'Speak up against racial discrimination, says Victorian Government', viewed 29 January 2019 https://www.sbs.com.au/yourlanguage/punjabi/en/article/2018/08/16/speak-against-racial-discrimination-says-victoria-government

2   Thomas Friedman, 'Order vs Disorder – Part 3', viewed 29 January 2019 https://www.nytimes.com/2014/08/24/opinion/sunday/thomas-l-friedman-order-vs-disorder-part-3.html

3   Kaya Yurieff, 'Facebook hits 2 billion monthly users', viewed on 27 January 2019 https://money.cnn.com/2017/06/27/technology/facebook-2-billion-users/index.html

4   'China lifting 800 million people out of poverty is historic: World Bank', viewed 29 January 2019 https://www.business-standard.com/article/international/china-lifting-800-million-people-out-of-poverty-is-historic-world-bank-117101300027_1.html

5   Cyndi Suarez, 'The Fragility of Cities and What to Do About It', viewed on 29 January 2019 https://nonprofitquarterly.org/2017/11/28/fragility-worlds-cities-affects-us/

6   'Climate vulnerable nations aim for 100 per cent renewable energy at talks in Marrakech', viewed 29 January 2019 https://www.google.com.au/amp/s/amp.smh.com.au/environment/climate-change/climate-vulnerable-nations-aim-for-100-per-cent-renewable-energy-at-talks-in-marrakech-20161119-gst5r9.html

7   Kate Connolly, 'G7 leaders agree to phase out fossil fuel use by end of century', viewed 29 January 2019 https://www.theguardian.com/world/2015/jun/08/g7-leaders-agree-phase-out-fossil-fuel-use-end-of-century

8   Thomas Friedman, 'Justice Goes Global', viewed on 29 January 2019 https://www.nytimes.com/subscription.html?campaignId=7QLQKandmtrref=www.google.com.auandgwh=50F49C12B25AF8388058ED2F838559D8andgwt=payandmktgrfr=gw_moband

9   'Human Proteome Project', viewed 29 January 2019 https://hupo.org/human-proteome-project

10   'Endangered languages', viewed on 29 January 2019 https://www.dandc.eu/en/article/indigenous-languages-have-immense-value

11   'There's more CO_2 in the atmosphere now than any point in almost a million years', viewed on 29 January 2019 https://www.pri.org/sto-

ries/2017-10-30/theres-more-co2-atmosphere-now-any-point-almost-million-years

12   'Hundreds of thousands affected by devastating floods in Peru', viewed on 29 January 2019 https://www.unicef.org/wash/peru_95467.html

13   'The Extinction Crisis', viewed on 29 January 2019 https://www.biologicaldiversity.org/programs/biodiversity/elements_of_biodiversity/extinction_crisis/

14   Ibid.

15   'Forced displacement above 68m in 2017, new global deal on refugees critical', viewed on 29 January 2019 https://www.unhcr.org/news/press/2018/6/5b27c2434/forced-displacedment-above-68m-2017-new-global-deal-refugees-critical.html

16   'UN Secretary General's Speech – 16 November 2017', viewed on 29 January 2019 https://www.un.org/sg/en/content/sg/statement/2017-11-16/secretary-general's-speech-soas-university-london-"counter-terrorism

17   Claire Mc Evoy and Gergely Hideg, 'Global Violent Deaths 2017: Time to Decide', viewed on 29 January 2019 http://www.smallarmssurvey.org/fileadmin/docs/U-Reports/SAS-Report-GVD2017.pdf

18   'Diabetes Globally', viewed on 29 January 2019 https://www.diabetesaustralia.com.au/diabetes-globally

19   'Suicide data', viewed on 29 January 2019 https://www.who.int/mental_health/prevention/suicide/suicideprevent/en/

20   Rupert Neate, 'Richest 1% own half the world's wealth, study finds', viewed on 29 January 2019 https://www.theguardian.com/inequality/2017/nov/14/worlds-richest-wealth-credit-suisse

21   Yuval Noah Harari, *Homo Deus: A Brief History of Tomorrow*, (Harvill Secker, London, 2015), 343.

22   Thomas Friedman, 'The unaccountable power of the digital revolution', viewed on 29 January 2019 https://gulfnews.com/opinion/op-eds/the-unaccountable-power-of-digital-revolution-1.2107039

23   'Democracy Index 2018', viewed on 29 January 2019 https://www.eiu.com/topic/democracy-index

24   'Franklin D. Roosevelt speaks of Four Freedoms', viewed on 29 January 2019 https://www.history.com/this-day-in-history/franklin-d-roosevelt-speaks-of-four-freedoms

25   'The Shanghai Cooperation Organization', viewed on 29 January 2019 https://www.cfr.org/backgrounder/shanghai-cooperation-organization

26   'Quadrilateral Security Dialogue', viewed on 29 January 2019 https://en.m.wikipedia.org/wiki/Quadrilateral_Security_Dialogue

27   Franklin Delano Roosevelt, 'Address at the Annual Dinner of the White House Correspondents' Associations 15 March 1941,' viewed 16 August 2018 http://www.fdrlibrary.marist.edu/mwg-internal/de5fs23hu73ds/progress?id=vJjQYAzjiXjRPYTAiccqjKtATJFU7hM8ZOw6O__o8xA,

28   Thomas Friedman, 'Can I Ruin Your Dinner Party?', viewed on 31 January 2019 www.google.com.au/amp/s/www.nytimes.com/2018/08/07/opinion/can-i-ruin-your-dinner-party.amp.html

29   Patrick Wintour, 'Russian bid to influence Brexit vote detailed in new US Senate report', viewed on www.google.com.au/amp/s/amp.theguardian.com/world/2018/jan/10/russian-influence-brexit-vote-detailed-us-senate-report

30   Thomas Friedman, 'Can I Ruin Your Dinner Party?', viewed on 31 January 2019 www.google.com.au/amp/s/www.nytimes.com/2018/08/07/opinion/can-i-ruin-your-dinner-party.amp.html

31   Ibid.

32   Walter Russell, 'Incredible Shrinking Europe', viewed on 28 February 2019, https://www.wsj.com/articles/incredible-shrinking-europe-11549928481< https://www.wsj.com/articles/incredible-shrinking-europe-11549928481>

33   'Trump to meet Kim at 9am Singapore time on 12 June, White House says', viewed on https://www.google.com.au/amp/s/amp.theguardian.com/world/2018/jun/04/trump-kim-nuclear-summit-singapore-white-house

34   Scott Neuman, 'North Korea Reportedly Expanding Ballistic Missile Production Facility', viewed on 31 January 2019 https://www.npr.org/2018/07/02/625267839/north-korea-reportedly-expanding-ballistic-missle-production-facility>

35   Thomas Friedman, 'Can I Ruin Your Dinner Party?', viewed on 31 January 2019 www.google.com.au/amp/s/www.nytimes.com/2018/08/07/opinion/can-i-ruin-your-dinner-party.amp.html

36   Sarah Joseph, 'As the US leaves the UN Human Rights Council, it may leave more damage in its wake', viewed on 31 January 2019 https://google.com.au/amp/s/theconversation.com/amp/as-the-us-leaves-the-un-human-rights-council-it-may-leave-more-damage-in-its-wake-98618

37   'Macron calls for multilateralism in rebuttal to Trump's isolationist UN speech', viewed on 31 January 2019 https://www.france24.com/en/20180925-macron-united-nations-general-assembly-speech-multilateralism-rebuttal-trump-iran

38   Ibid.

39   'The Shanghai Cooperation Organization', viewed on 29 January 2019 https://www.cfr.org/backgrounder/shanghai-cooperation-organization

40   Ibid.

41   Matt Schiavenza, 'How Humiliation Drove Modern Chinese History', viewed on 31 January 2019 https://www.theatlantic.com/china/archive/2013/10/how-humiliation-drove-modern-chinese-history/280878/

42   Ibid.

43   'Xi Jinping and the Chinese Dream', viewed on 31 January 2019 https://www.dw.com/en/xi-jinping-and-the-chinese-dream/a-43685630

44   Ibid.

45   '2017 Foreign Policy White Paper', viewed on 31 January 2019 https://www.fpwhitepaper.gov.au

46   Ibid.

47   'The World in 2050: The long view: how will the global economic order change by 2050?', viewed on 31 January 2019 https://www.pwc.com/gx/en/issues/economy/the-world-in-2050.html

48   'Sharp Power: Rising Authoritarian Influence: New Forum Report – 5 December 2017' viewed on 31 January 2019 https://www.ned.org/sharp-power-rising-authoritarian-influence-forum-report/

49   'Sharp Power: Rising Authoritarian Influence: New Forum Report – 5 December 2017' viewed on 31 January 2019 https://www.ned.org/sharp-power-rising-authoritarian-influence-forum-report/

50   Ibid.

51   Ted S Yoho, 'China's Second Century of Humiliation', viewed on 18 January 2019 https://thediplomat.com/2018/06/chinas-second-century-of-humiliation/

52   Vicky Xiuzhong Xu and Bang Xiao, 'China's Social Credit System seeks to assign citizens scores, engineer social behaviour', viewed on 1 February 2019 https://www.abc.net.au/news/2018-03-31/chinas-social-credit-system-punishes-untrustworthy-citizens/9596204

53 'Jointly Building the Belt and Road for Win-Win Development', viewed 1 February 2019 https://www.fmprc.gov.cn/mfa_eng/wjb_663304/zwjg_665342/zwbd_665378/t1616699.shtml

54 'China's Belt and Road Initiative: Debt trap or hope?', viewed on 1 February 2019 https://www.straitstimes.com/asia/east-asia/chinas-belt-and-road-initiative-debt-trap-or-hope

55 Brendon Hong, 'China's Plans For World Conquest? Easy Credit', viewed on 1 February 2019 < https://www.thedailybeast.com/chinas-plans-for-easy-credit-world-conquest

56 Ibid.

57 Ibid.

58 Ibid.

59 Ibid.

60 Ibid.

61 Michael J Green, 'The Legacy of Obama's "Pivot" to Asia', viewed on 1 February 2019, < https://foreignpolicy.com/2016/09/03/the-legacy-of-obamas-pivot-to-asia/

62 'Beijing set to pledge billions more for Africa despite concerns over Chinese lending', viewed on 1 February 2019 < https://www.scmp.com/news/china/diplomacy/article/2162341/beijing-set-pledge-billions-more-africa-despite-concerns-over

63 Ibid.

64 'The Role of U.N. Peacekeeping in China's Expanding Strategic Interests', viewed on 1 February 2019 https://www.usip.org/publications/2018/09/role-un-peacekeeping-chinas-expanding-strategic-interests

65 Thomas Friedman, 'What if Trump Did Actually Shoot Someone on Fifth Avenue?', viewed on 1 February 2019 < https://www.nytimes.com/2018/08/28/opinion/trump-midterms-shoot-fifth-avenue.html

66 Christopher Ashley Ford, 'Why China Technology-Transfer Threats Matter', viewed on 1 February 2019 < https://www.state.gov/t/isn/rls/rm/2018/286889.htm

67 Moises Naim, 'The Uprising of the Global Middle Class', viewed 3 February 2019, https://www.moisesnaim.com/columns/2017/8/29/the-uprising-of-the-global-middle-class

68 Homi Kharas, 'The Unprecedented Expansion of the Global Middle Class', viewed 9 February 2019, https://www.brookings.edu/wp-content/uploads/2017/02/global_20170228_global-middle-class.pdf

69   'Poverty', viewed 8 February 2019, https://www.worldbank.org/en/topic/poverty/overview

70   'Warren Introduces Accountable Capitalism Act', viewed on 9 February 2019, https://www.warren.senate.gov/newsroom/press-releases/warren-introduces-accountable-capitalism-act

71   'World Economic Outlook Update, July 2018', viewed 9 February 2019, https://www.imf.org/en/Publications/WEO/Issues/2018/07/02/world-economic-outlook-update-july-2018

72   Huileng Tan and Yen Nee Lee, 'China reports economic growth below expectations — its worst pace since the financial crisis', viewed 9 February 2019, https://www.cnbc.com/2018/10/19/china-q3-gdp-china-posts-economic-data-amid-trade-war-with-us.html

73   Ibid.

74   Nouriel Roubini and Brunello Rosa, 'Nouriel Roubini, who foresaw the financial crisis is one who believes the US may be heading for a recession on 2020', viewed on 9 February 2019, https://www.theguardian.com/business/2018/sep/13/recession-2020-financial-crisis-nouriel-roubini

75   Enda Curran, 'China's Debt Bomb', viewed 8 February 2019, https://www.bloomberg.com/quicktake/chinas-debt-bomb

76   'Cause for Concern? The top 10 risks to the global economy 2019', viewed on 28 February 2019, https://www.eiu.com/public/topical_report.aspx?campaignid=GlobalRisks2019

77   'Hal Harvey's Insights And Updates – The Real Deal In Abating Climate Change: Four Zeros', viewed 11 February 2019, https://energyinnovation.org/2017/11/29/hal-harveys-insights-updates-real-deal-abating-climate-change-four-zeros/

78   Devan Cole and Sunlen Serfaty, 'Ocasio-Cortez and Markey unveil Green New Deal resolution', viewed on 11 February 2019, https://edition.cnn.com/2019/02/07/politics/alexandria-ocasio-cortez-ed-markey-green-new-deal/index.html

79   Naomi Klein, 'The Game-Changing Promise of a Green New Deal', viewed on 11 February 2019, https://theintercept.com/2018/11/27/green-new-deal-congress-climate-change/

80   Ibid.

81   Rob Smith, 'Three countries are leading the renewable energy revolution', viewed on 11 February 2019, https://www.weforum.org/agenda/2018/02/countries-behind-global-renewable-energy-growth/

82 Ellie Donnelly, 'More than a third of Irish electricity to be green within four years', viewed on 11 February 2019, https://www.independent.ie/au/business/irish/more-than-a-third-of-irish-electricity-to-be-green-within-four-years-36746874.html

83 Ibid.

84 'India's renewable energy capacity to double by 2022, report says', viewed on 11 February 2019, https://www.hindustantimes.com/environment/india-s-renewable-energy-capacity-to-double-by-2022-report-says/story-9YFGwdg1PdHmQTFKLGgDTJ.html

85 'Internet World Stats', viewed on 11 February 2019, https://www.internetworldstats.com/stats.htm

86 Matthew Carney, 'Leave No Dark Corner', viewed on 11 February 2019, https://www.abc.net.au/news/2018-09-18/china-social-credit-a-model-citizen-in-a-digital-dictatorship/10200278

87 Angus Grigg, 'No such thing as a private company in China: FIRB', viewed 11 February 2019, https://www.afr.com/news/policy/foreign-investment/no-such-thing-as-a-private-company-in-china-firb-20190116-h1a4ut

88 'Transistor', viewed 11 February 2019, https://www.britannica.com/technology/transistor ; 'A Brief History of the Digital Revolution', viewed 11 February 2019, https://stfc.ukri.org/files/digital-revolution-infographic/

89 Ibid.

90 Ibid.

91 Ibid.

92 'The Spectator Index', viewed on 11 February 2019, https://twitter.com/spectatorindex/status/1021273705589231616

93 'The Spectator Index', viewed on 11 February 2019, https://twitter.com/spectatorindex/status/1001908606445355009>

94 Yuval Harari, 'Why Technology Favors Tyranny', viewed on 8 February 2019, https://www.theatlantic.com/magazine/archive/2018/10/yuval-noah-harari-technology-tyranny/568330/

95 Jessica Murphy, 'Trudeau gives Canada first cabinet with equal number of men and women', viewed 9 February 2019, https://www.theguardian.com/world/2015/nov/04/canada-cabinet-gender-diversity-justin-trudeau

96 'Dmitry Medvedev's Second Cabinet', viewed on 9 February 2019, https://en.wikipedia.org/wiki/Dmitry_Medvedev%27s_Second_Cabinet;

'Li Keqiang Government', viewed on 9 February 2019, https://en.wikipedia.org/wiki/Li_Keqiang_Government

97 'Reality Check: Does China's Communist Party have a woman problem?', viewed on 9 February 2019, https://www.bbc.com/news/world-asia-41652487

98 'SDG 5: Achieve gender equality and empower all women and girls', viewed 9 February 2019, http://www.unwomen.org/en/news/in-focus/women-and-the-sdgs/sdg-5-gender-equality

99 'Violence against women', viewed on 2 February 2019 https://www.who.int/news-room/fact-sheets/detail/violence-against-women

100 Nick Baker, 'Child marriage declines globally but millions still marrying young', viewed on 2 February 2019 https://www.sbs.com.au/news/child-marriage-declines-globally-but-millions-still-marrying-young

101 Biwa Kwan, 'More than half of women killed in 2017 died at hands of partner or relative', viewed on 2 February 2019 https://www.sbs.com.au/news/more-than-half-of-women-killed-in-2017-died-at-hands-of-partner-or-relative

102 'Life expectancy at birth', viewed on 2 February 2019 https://data.worldbank.org/indicator/SP.DYN.LE00.IN

103 'Millennium Development Goals (MDGs)', viewed on 2 February 2019 https://www.who.int/news-room/fact-sheets/detail/millennium-development-goals-(mdgs)

104 'Human Proteome Project', viewed 29 January 2019 https://hupo.org/human-proteome-project

105 Meghan Rabbitt, 'The 10 Most Incredible Medical Breakthroughs of 2018', viewed on 2 February 2019 https://www.google.com/health/gmp25423574/top-medical-breakthroughs/

106 Anthony White, 'AMP 2018: Improving patient selection through precision medicine', viewed on 2 February 2019, https://planetinnovation.com/amp-2018-improving-patient-selection-through-precision-medicine/

107 'World Health Organisation', viewed on 2 February 2019 <https://www.who.int/bulletin/volumes/95/9/16-189977/en/>

108 Yuval Noah Harari, 'Why Technology Favors Tyranny', viewed on 2 February 2019 https://amp.theatlantic.com/amp/article/568330/

109 'Directory of United Nations System Organisations', viewed on 2 February 2019 https://www.unsystem.org/members/specialized-agencies

110 Ibid.

111 Joby Warrick and Chris Mooney, '196 countries approve historic climate agreement', viewed on 2 February 2019 https://www.washingtonpost.com/news/energy-environment/wp/2015/12/12/proposed-historic-climate-pact-nears-final-vote/?noredirect=onandutm_term=.a8d94fc73912

112 Suzanne Goldenberg, 'Climate Change: Will '1.5 to stay alive' deal be enough to save Seychelles', viewed on 2 February 2019 https://www.theguardian.com/environment/2015/dec/12/climate-change-seychelles-cop21-economy-collapse

113 Bill McKibben, 'How Extreme Weather is Shrinking the Planet', viewed on 2 February 2019 https://www.newyorker.com/magazine/2018/11/26/how-extreme-weather-is-shrinking-the-planet

114 Damian Carrington, 'Humanity has wiped out 60 per cent of animal populations since 1970, report finds', viewed on 2 February 2019 https://www.theguardian.com/environment/2018/oct/30/humanity-wiped-out-animals-since-1970-major-report-finds

115 'Living Planet Report 2018: Aiming higher', viewed 2 February 2019 https://wwf.panda.org/knowledge_hub/all_publications/living_planet_report_2018/

116 Ibid.

117 Edward O. Wilson, *Half Earth: Our Planet's Fight for Life*, (Liveright Publishing Corporation, London, 2016), 3.

118 Philip Levy, 'Was letting China Into the WTO a Mistake', viewed on 2 February 2019, https://www.foreignaffairs.com/articles/china/2018-04-02/was-letting-china-wto-mistake

119 'China lifting 800 million people out of poverty is historic: World Bank', viewed 29 January 2019 https://www.business-standard.com/article/international/china-lifting-800-million-people-out-of-poverty-is-historic-world-bank-117101300027_1.html

120 'China in the WTO: Past, Present and Future', viewed 2 February 2019, https://www.wto.org/english/thewto_e/acc_e/s7lu_e.pdf

121 Angus Grigg, 'No such thing as a private company in China: FIRB', viewed on 2 February 2019 https://www.afr.com/news/policy/foreign-investment/no-such-thing-as-a-private-company-in-china-firb-20190116-h1a4ut

122 Peter Navarro, 'China must stop forcing US firms to share intellectual property', viewed 2 February 2019 https://www.google.com.au/amp/s/amp.usatoday.com/amp/563151001

123 Ibid.

124 'Market Capitalization of the biggest internet companies worldwide as of May 2018', viewed on 2 February 2019, https://www.statista.com/statistics/277483/market-value-of-the-largest-internet-companies-world-wide/

125 Graham Allison, 'Is war between China and the US inevitable', viewed on 2 February 2019 https://www.ted.com/talks/graham_allison_is_war_between_china_and_the_us_inevitable/transcript?language=en

126 Christopher Knaus, 'Greed the common thread in scandals played out at bank royal commission', viewed on 2 February 2019 https://www.theguardian.com/australia-news/2019/feb/01/greed-the-common-thread-in-scandals-played-out-at-bank-royal-commission

127 'Member Nations', viewed on 3 February 2019, https://www.nato.int/cps/em/natohq/topics_52044.htm

128 Ibid.

129 'Forced displacement above 68m in 2017, new global deal on refugees critical', viewed on 29 January 2019 https://www.unhcr.org/news/press/2018/6/5b27c2434/forced-displacedment-above-68m-2017-new-global-deal-refugees-critical.html

130 'Report of the United Nations High Commissioner for Refugees: Global compact on refugees', viewed on 3 February 2019, https://www.un.org/en/conf/migration/global-compact-for-safe-orderly-regular-migration.shtml

131 'Draft Outcome Document of the Conference', https://undocs.org/A/CONF.231/3

132 'Nothing to lose: PM refusal to sign UN migration compact criticised', viewed on 3 February 2019, https://www.sbs.com.au/yourlanguage/spanish/en/article/2018/11/21/nothing-lose-pm-refusal-sign-un-migration-compact-criticised

133 Danielle Kurtzleben, 'A Record Number of Women Will Serve In Congress', viewed 3 February 2019, https://www.npr.org/2018/11/07/665019211/a-record-number-of-women-will-serve-in-congress-with-potentially-more-to-come

134 Wenshan Jia, 'China's "Belt and Road Initiative" is good for the world, despite what Western critics say', viewed on 3 February 2019, https://www.google.com.au/amp/s/amp.scmp.com/comment/insight-opinion/article/2136325/chinas-belt-and-road-initiative-good-world-despite-what

135 Jack Kilbride, 'What's in Victoria's controversial One Belt One Road agreement with China?', viewed on 3 February 2019 https://www.google.com.au/amp/amp.abc.net.au/article/10486996

136 William Morris, 'Thomas Friedman: Society should mimic nature to thrive', viewed on 3 February 2019, https://finance-commerce.com/2018/04/thomas-friedman-society-should-mimic-nature-to-thrive/; Thomas Friedman, 'Has Our Luck Run Out?', viewed on 1 May 2019, <https://www.nytimes.com/2019/04/30/opinion/trump-climate-change.html>

137 Tom Huston, 'How do we feed the planet in 2050', viewed on 3 February 2019, https://www.theguardian.com/preparing-for-9-billion/2017/sep/13/population-feed-planet-2050-cold-chain-environment

138 Sir Ken Robinson, 'Schools kill creativity', viewed on 3 February 2019, https://www.ted.com/talks/ken_robinson_says_schools_kill_creativity

139 Avneet Aroram 'Speak up against racial discrimination, says Victorian Government', viewed 29 January 2019 https://www.sbs.com.au/yourlanguage/punjabi/en/article/2018/08/16/speak-against-racial-discrimination-says-victoria-government

140 David Chau, 'Huawei lashes out at "malicious" and "unfair" treatment by Australia and other nations', viewed on 3 February 2019, https://www.abc.net.au/news/2018-12-28/huawei-lashes-out-at-unfair-treatment-australia-western-nations/10671818

141 'Choose your country or region', viewed on 3 February 2019, https://www.apple.com/choose-country-region/

142 Ronald Mizen, 'The BBC's Jamie Angus talks soft power, fake news and the global information war', viewed on 3 February 2019, https://www.afr.com/business/media-and-marketing/tv/the-bbcs-jamie-angus-talks-soft-power-fake-news-and-the-global-information-war-20180910-h1579j

143 "$41 million slated for Aust space agency', viewed on 3 February 2019, https://www.sbs.com.au/news/41-million-slated-for-aust-space-agency?cid=newsapp:socialshare:copylink

144 'Why Australia', viewed 3 February 2019, https://www.austrade.gov.au/ArticleDocuments/3823/Australia-Benchmark-Report.pdf.aspx

145 'List of government space agencies', viewed on 3 February 2019, https://en.m.wikipedia.org/wiki/List_of_government_space_agencies

146 Ibid.

147 Ibid.

148 Simon Thomsen, 'Elon Musk wants to fly people around the world in under an hour', viewed on 3 February 2019, https://www.google.com.au/amp/s/amp.businessinsider.com/elon-musk-wants-to-fly-people-around-the-world-in-under-an-hour-2017-9

149 Ibid.

150 'List of government space agencies', viewed on 3 February 2019, https://en.m.wikipedia.org/wiki/List_of_government_space_agencies

151 'Global Parliamentary Report', viewed on 3 February 2019, http://archive.ipu.org/gpr-e/media/index.htm

152 Moises Naim, 'The Uprising of the Global Middle Class', viewed 3 February 2019, https://www.theatlantic.com/international/archive/2017/08/global-middle-class-discontent/535581/

153 Simon Rogers, 'Bobby Kennedy on GDP: "measures everything except that which is worthwhile"', viewed on 3 February 2019, https://www.google.com.au/amp/s/amp.theguardian.com/news/datablog/2012/may/24/robert-kennedy-gdp

154 'Sharp Power: Rising Authoritarian Influence: New Forum Report – 5 December 2017' viewed on 31 January 2019 https://www.ned.org/sharp-power-rising-authoritarian-influence-forum-report/

155 Gordon Rose, 'The Fourth Founding and The Liberal Order', *Foreign Affairs,* viewed on 3 March 2019, <https://www.foreignaffairs.com/articles/united-states/2018-12-11/fourth-founding>

156 'Quick Study: Moises Niam on power – It ain't what it used to be', viewed on 3 February 2019, https://www.economist.com/blogs/prospero/2013/03/quick-study-moises-na%C3%ADm-power

157 'The Paris Agreement', viewed on 3 February 2019, https://unfccc.int/process-and-meetings/the-paris-agreement/the-paris-agreement

158 Ibid.

159 'Donald Trump: Washington formally tells UN of Paris agreement withdrawal', viewed on 4 February 2019, https://mobile.abc.net.au/news/2017-08-05/trump:-us-formally-tells-un-of-withdrawal-from-paris-agreement/8777420

160 'The Paris Agreement', viewed on 3 February 2019, https://unfccc.int/process-and-meetings/the-paris-agreement/the-paris-agreement

161 Oliver Milman, 'Last year was warmest ever that didn't feature an El Nino, report finds', viewed 4 February 2019, https://www.google.com.

au/amp/s/amp.theguardian.com/environment/2018/aug/01/state-of-the-climate-report-noaa-2017-third-warmest

162 Ibid.

163 'Global Climate Report – Annual 2017', viewed on 11 February 2019, < https://www.ncdc.noaa.gov/sotc/global/201713>

164 Ibid.

165 Ibid.

166 Ibid.

167 Ibid.

168 Ibid.

169 Ibid.

170 'El Niño did not influence global climate in 2017, but still anomalies are sobering', viewed on 11 February 2019, https://www.downtoearth.org.in/news/climate-change/climate-change-and-wildfires-how-do-we-know-if-there-is-a-link--61374

171 Ibid.

172 Ibid.

173 Ibid.

174 'Global Climate Report – Annual 2017', viewed on 11 February 2019, https://www.ncdc.noaa.gov/sotc/global/201713

175 'Heat: the next big inequality issue', viewed on 12 February 2019, https://www.theguardian.com/cities/2018/aug/13/heat-next-big-in-equality-issue-heatwaves-world

176 Alejandra Borunda, 'Are Europe's Historic Fires Caused by Climate Change', viewed on 4 February 2019, https://www.nationalgeographic.com/environment/2018/07/are-fires-in-europe-the-result-of-climate-change-/

177 Ibid.

178 Jungeun Kim, 'Record-breaking temperatures leave 29 dead in South Korea heatwave', viewed 4 February 2019, https://www.google.com.au/amp/s/amp.cnn.com/cnn/2018/08/02/asia/south-korea-heatwave-deaths-intl/index.html

179 'Death toll rises to 91 in deadly Greece wildfire', viewed on 4 February 2019, https://www.google.com.au/amp/s/www.cbsnews.com/amp/news/death-toll-rises-deadly-greece-wildfires-today-2018-07-29/

180 'Europe heatwave: Spain and Portugal struggle in 40C+ temperatures', viewed on 4 February 2019, https://www.bbc.com/news/amp/world-europe-45070498

181 Rebecca Lindsay, 'Climate Change: Atmospheric Carbon Dioxide', viewed on 4 February 2019, https://www.climate.gov/news-features/understanding-climate/climate-change-atmospheric-carbon-dioxide

182 Robert Rapier, 'Oil Company Spending And Oil Reserves Are On the Rise', viewed 4 February 2019, https://www.forbes.com/sites/rrapier/2018/07/27/oil-company-spending-and-oil-reserves-are-on-the-rise/amp/

183 'Investment in Renewables Dropped 7 per cent Globally in 2017', viewed on 4 February 2019, https://e360.yale.edu/digest/investment-in-renewables-dropped-7-percent-globally-in-2017

184 'Coral reefs losing ability to keep pace with sea level rise', viewed on 4 February 2019, https://www.coralcoe.org.au/media-releases/coral-reefs-losing-ability-to-keep-pace-with-sea-level-rise

185 Ibid.

186 Jen Mills, 'Europe facing its hottest day ever as heatwave hits with 48C heat on its way', viewed 4 February 2019, https://metro.co.uk/2018/08/01/europe-facing-hottest-day-ever-heatwave-hits-48C-heatway-7784431/amp/

187 Ibid.

188 Ibid.

189 Ibid.

190 '68% of the world population projected to live in urban areas by 2050, says UN', viewed on 13 February 2019, https://www.un.org/development/desa/en/news/population/2018-revision-of-world-urbanization-prospects.html

191 'Heat: the next big inequality issue', viewed on 13 February 2019, < https://www.theguardian.com/cities/2018/aug/13/heat-next-big-inequality-issue-heatwaves-world>

192 Ibid.

193 Ibid.

194 Ibid.

195 Ibid.

196 Ibid.

197 Thomas Friedman, 'What if Mother Nature Is on the Ballot in 2020?', viewed on 13 February 2019, https://www.nytimes.com/2018/08/14/opinion/2020-election-climate-change-trump.html

198 Ibid.

199 Ibid.

200 Ibid.

201 Yuval Noah Harari, *21 Lessons for the 21st Century* (Jonathan Cape, London, 2018), x.

202 John Kerry, 'John Kerry: Forget Trump. We All Must Act on Climate Change', viewed on 12 February 2019, https://www.nytimes.com/2018/12/13/opinion/kerry-climate-change-trump.html

203 'Living Planet Report 2018', viewed on 12 February 2019, https://www.worldwildlife.org/pages/living-planet-report-2018

204 Ibid.

205 Rupert Neate, 'Richest 1% own half the world's wealth, study finds', viewed on 29 January 2019 https://www.theguardian.com/inequality/2017/nov/14/worlds-richest-wealth-credit-suisse

206 'The rich, the poor and the growing gap between them', viewed on 13 February 2019, https://www.economist.com/special-report/2006/06/15/the-rich-the-poor-and-the-growing-gap-between-them

207 'How Come There Are So Many Billionaires in Communist China?', viewed on 13 February 2019, https://www.bloomberg.com/news/articles/2018-11-29/why-communist-china-is-home-to-so-many-billionaires-quicktake

208 Ibid.

209 Ibid.

210 Shaun Walker, 'Unequal Russia: is anger stirring in the global capital of inequality?', viewed on 13 February 2019, https://www.theguardian.com/inequality/2017/apr/25/unequal-russia-is-anger-stirring-in-the-global-capital-of-inequality

211 Gareth Hutchens, 'IMF says Australia has one of the fastest rising income inequality rates', viewed on 13 February 2019, https://www.theguardian.com/business/2017/oct/12/imf-says-australia-has-one-of-the-fastest-rising-income-inequality-rates

212 'Australian billionaires richer than the bottom fifth of the population', viewed 13 February 2019, https://www.sbs.com.au/news/australian-billionaires-richer-than-the-bottom-fifth-of-the-population

213 Yuval Noah Harari, *21 Lessons for the 21st Century* (Jonathan Cape, London, 2018), 75.

214 Thomas Piketty, *Capital In the Twenty-First Century*, (The Belknap Press of Harvard University Press, Cambridge, 2014), 518.

215 '5 shocking facts about extreme global inequality and how to even it up', viewed on 19 February 2019, https://www.oxfam.org/en/even-it/5-shocking-facts-about-extreme-global-inequality-and-how-even-it-davos

216 Neal Gabler, 'The Secret Shame of Middle-Class Americans', viewed on 13 February 2019, https://www.theatlantic.com/magazine/archive/2016/05/my-secret-shame/476415/

217 Matthew Yglesias, 'Elizabeth Warren has a plan to save capitalism', viewed 13 February 2019, https://www.vox.com/2018/8/15/17683022/elizabeth-warren-accountable-capitalism-corporations

218 'UN Secretary General's Speech - 16 November 2017', viewed on 29 January 2019 https://www.un.org/sg/en/content/sg/statement/2017-11-16/secretary-general's-speech-soas-university-london-"counter-terrorism

219 Yuval Noah Harari, *21 Lessons for the 21st Century* (Jonathan Cape, London, 2018), xi.

220 Ben Jacobs, 'America since 9/11: timeline of attacks linked to the "war on terror"', viewed on 13 February 2019, https://www.theguardian.com/us-news/2017/nov/01/america-since-911-terrorist-attacks-linked-to-the-war-on-terror

221 Ibid.

222 'Lists of Terrorist Incidents in 2015', viewed on 13 February 2019, https://en.wikipedia.org/wiki/List_of_terrorist_incidents_in_2015

223 'Lists of Terrorists Incidents in 2016', viewed on 13 February 2019, https://en.wikipedia.org/wiki/List_of_terrorist_incidents_in_2016

224 'Lists of Terrorists Incidents in 2017', viewed on 13 February 2019, https://en.wikipedia.org/wiki/List_of_terrorist_incidents_in_2017

225 'Lists of Terrorists Incidents in 2018', viewed on 13 February 2019, https://en.wikipedia.org/wiki/List_of_terrorist_incidents_in_2018

226 Ali Soufan, *Anatomy of Terror* (W.W Norton and Company, New York, 2018), xvi.

227 Ibid, 296 and 297.

228 'Melbourne shooting: Man being investigated over terrorism shot dead after stabbing police officers outside Endeavour Hills police station',

viewed on 8 February 2019, https://www.abc.net.au/news/2014-09-23/
one-person-shot-dead-two-stabbed-endeavour-hills/5764408

229 Parramatta Shootings, 'https://www.theguardian.com/australia-news/
parramatta-shooting', viewed on 8 February 2019, https://www.theguard-
ian.com/australia-news/parramatta-shooting

230 'Completed Inquires and Reports', viewed on 8 February 2019, https://
www.aph.gov.au/Parliamentary_Business/Committees/Joint/Intelligence_
and_Security/Completed_inquiries

231 Hannah Ritchie, 'What do people die from?', viewed on 8 February 2019,
https://ourworldindata.org/what-does-the-world-die-from

232 'German parliament foiled cyber attack by hackers via Israeli website',
viewed on 8 February 2019, https://www.reuters.com/article/us-germa-
ny-cyber-idUSKBN1701V3

233 Taylor Armerding, 'The OPM breach report: A long time coming', viewed
8 February 2019, https://www.csoonline.com/article/3130682/da-
ta-breach/the-opm-breach-report-a-long-time-coming.html

234 Stephanie Borys, 'Russian hacking: Up to 400 Australian companies caught
up in cyber attacks blamed on Moscow', viewed on 8 February 2019,
https://www.abc.net.au/news/2018-04-17/australians-caught-up-in-cy-
ber-attacks-blamed-on-russia/9665820

235 Yuval Harari, 'Why Technology Favors Tyranny', viewed on 8 February
2019, https://www.theatlantic.com/magazine/archive/2018/10/yu-
val-noah-harari-technology-tyranny/568330/

236 'Forced displacement above 68m in 2017, new global deal on refugees
critical', viewed on 29 January 2019 https://www.unhcr.org/news/
press/2018/6/5b27c2434/forced-displacedment-above-68m-2017-new-
global-deal-refugees-critical.html

237 'Syria Emergency', viewed on 13 February 2019, https://www.unhcr.org/
syria-emergency.html

238 'Emergencies', viewed on 13 February 2019, https://www.unhcr.org/
emergencies.html

239 Ibid.

240 'Migrant crisis: One million enter Europe in 2015', viewed on 13 February
2019, https://www.bbc.com/news/world-europe-35158769

241 'The Sahara Desert is expanding', viewed on 13 February 2019, https://
www.sciencedaily.com/releases/2018/03/180329141035.htm

242 Ibid.

243 Laignee Barron, '143 Million People Could Soon Be Displaced Because of Climate Change, World Bank Says,' *Time*, 20 March 2018.

244 Jessica Meyers, 'China once welcomed refugees, but its policies now make Trump look lenient', viewed on 13 February 2019, https://www.latimes.com/world/asia/la-fg-china-forgotten-refugees-2017108-story.html

245 Ibid.

246 'Russian Federation', viewed on 13 February 2019, http://reporting.unhcr.org/node/2551

247 Ben Doherty, 'Australia takes the most refugees since start of humanitarian program', viewed on 13 February 2019, https://www.theguardian.com/world/2018/feb/10/australia-takes-the-most-refugees-since-start-of-humanitarian-program

248 'Intergovernmental Conference on the Global Compact for Migration', viewed on 13 February 2019, http://www.un.org/en/conf/migration/

249 Kathryn Perrot, '"Fake news" on social media influenced US election voters, experts say', viewed on 18 February 2019, https://www.abc.net.au/news/2016-11-14/fake-news-would-have-influenced-us-election-experts-say/8024660

250 Yuval Harari, 'Why Technology Favors Tyranny', viewed on 8 February 2019, https://www.theatlantic.com/magazine/archive/2018/10/yuval-noah-harari-technology-tyranny/568330/

251 'Suicide data', viewed on 29 January 2019 https://www.who.int/mental_health/prevention/suicide/suicideprevent/en/

252 Yuval Harari, 'Yuval Noah Harari on what the year 2050 has in store for humankind', viewed on 8 February 2019, https://www.wired.co.uk/article/yuval-noah-harari-extract-21-lessons-for-the-21st-century

253 Yuval Harari, 'Why Technology Favors Tyranny', viewed on 8 February 2019, https://www.theatlantic.com/magazine/archive/2018/10/yuval-noah-harari-technology-tyranny/568330/

254 Ibid.

255 'Modernization of nuclear weapons continues; number of peacekeepers declines: New SIPRI Yearbook out now', viewed 8 February 2019, https://www.sipri.org/media/press-release/2018/modernization-nuclear-weapons-continues-number-peacekeepers-declines-new-sipri-yearbook-out-now

256 Ibid.

257 Ibid.

258 Julian Borger and Ian Sample, 'Which countries have nuclear weapons?', viewed on 8 February 2019, https://www.theguardian.com/world/2018/jul/16/nuclear-war-north-korea-russia-what-will-happen-how-likely-explained

259 'Nobel Peace Prize 2017', viewed 8 February 2019, http://www.icanw.org/action/nobel-peace-prize-2017-2/

260 Ibid.

261 'Donald Trump confirms US withdrawal from INF nuclear treaty', viewed 8 February 2019, https://www.theguardian.com/world/2019/feb/01/inf-donald-trump-confirms-us-withdrawal-nuclear-treaty

262 Sean Fleming, 'What are the whereabouts of the world's nuclear weapons?', viewed on 8 February 2019, < https://www.weforum.org/agenda/2018/10/chart-of-the-day-where-are-the-world-s-nuclear-weapons/>

263 'Trump Kim summit: US and North Korean leaders hold historic talks', viewed on 8 February 2019, https://www.bbc.com/news/world-asia-44435035

264 'North Korea says it will not denuclearize unless US removes "threat"', viewed on 8 February 2019, https://www.theguardian.com/world/2018/dec/20/north-korea-us-kim-jong-un-trump-denuclearize-nuclear-threat

265 Ibid.

266 Ibid.

267 Hans M. Kristensen and Robert S. Norris, 'Status of World Nuclear Forces', viewed on 8 February 2019, https://fas.org/issues/nuclear-weapons/status-world-nuclear-forces/

268 'Sharp Power: Rising Authoritarian Influence: New Forum Report – 5 December 2017' viewed on 31 January 2019 https://www.ned.org/sharp-power-rising-authoritarian-influence-forum-report/

269 'What are Confucius Classrooms and why are they being reviewed in NSW?', viewed on 8 February 2019, https://www.sbs.com.au/news/what-are-confucius-classrooms-and-why-are-they-being-reviewed-in-nsw

270 'Chinese Influence and American Interest', viewed on 8 February 2019, https://asiasociety.org/sites/default/files/inline-files/ChineseInfluence-AndAmericaninterests_Report_11.29.2018.pdf

271 Orville Schell and Larry Diamond, 'China Gets Its Message to Americans but Doesn't Want to Reciprocate', viewed on 8 February 2019, https://www.wsj.com/articles/china-gets-its-message-to-americans-but-doesnt-want-to-reciprocate-11545407490; Orville Schell and Larry Diamond,

'Chinese Influence and American Interests', viewed on 8 February 2019, https://asiasociety.org/sites/default/files/inline-files/ChineseInfluence-AndAmericaninterests_Report_11.29.2018.pdf

272 'Background to "Assessing Russian Activities and Intentions in Recent US Elections": The Analytic Process and Cyber Incident Attribution', viewed on 8 February 2019, https://www.dni.gov/files/documents/ICA_2017_01.pdf

273 'Apple, Amazon deny Bloomberg report on Chinese hardware attack', viewed on 8 February 2019, https://www.reuters.com/article/us-chi-na-cyber/apple-amazon-deny-bloomberg-report-on-chinese-hardware-at-tack-idUSKCN1ME19J

274 Clive Hamilton, *Silent Invasion: China's Influence in Australia* (Hardie Grants Books, Melbourne, 2018), backcover.

275 Ursula Malone, 'Chinese businessman Huang Xiangmo's political donations revealed; parties "too reliant"', viewed on 13 February 2019, https://www.abc.net.au/news/2017-12-12/huang-xiangmos-develop-ment-linked-to-greater-sydney-commission/9247860

276 Dan Harrison, 'Victorian Government releases agreement with China on Belt and Road Initiative', viewed 13 February 2019, https://www.abc.net.au/news/2018-11-12/victoria-china-belt-and-road-infrastruc-ture-agreement-released/10487034

277 Clive Hamilton, *Silent Invasion: China's Influence in Australia* (Hardie Grants Books, Melbourne, 2018), 103.

278 Chris Uhlmann, 'Chinese investment in Australia's power grid explained', viewed on 13 February 2019, https://www.abc.net.au/news/2016-08-21/chinese-investment-in-the-australian-power-grid/7766086

279 Helen Davidson, 'Chinese company secures 99-year lease of Darwin port in $506m deal', viewed on 13 February 2019, https://www.theguardian.com/australia-news/2015/oct/13/chinese-company-secures-99-year-lease-of-darwin-port-in-506m-deal

280 Nick McKenzie, Richard Baker, Chris Uhlmann, 'Liberal Andrew Robb took $880k China job as soon as he left Parliament', viewed on 13 February 2019, https://www.smh.com.au/national/liberal-andrew-robb-took-880k-china-job-as-soon-as-he-left-parliament-20170602-gwje3e.html

281 Kelvin Chan and Rob Gillies, 'Huawei, accused of violating US sanctions, uses soft sporting power to win favour', viewed on 13 February 2019, https://www.afr.com/news/politics/world/huawei-accused-of-violating-us-sanctions-uses-soft-sporting-power-to-win-favour-20190214-h1b8is

282 Clive Hamilton, *Silent Invasion: China's Influence in Australia* (Hardie Grants Books, Melbourne, 2018), 154-155.

283 David Wroe and Chris Uhlmann, 'Australia's major political parties hacked in "sophisticated" attack ahead of election', viewed on 26 February 2019, https://www.smh.com.au/politics/federal/australia-s-major-political-parties-hacked-in-sophisticated-attack-ahead-of-election-20190218-p50yi1.html

284 Bevan Shields, 'ASIO chief Duncan Lewis sounds fresh alarm over foreign interference threat', viewed on 14 February 2019, https://www.smh.com.au/politics/federal/asio-chief-duncan-lewis-sounds-fresh-alarm-over-foreign-interference-threat-20180524-p4zhdk.html

285 'Foreign Influence Transparency Scheme Bill 2018', viewed on 13 February 2019, https://www.aph.gov.au/Parliamentary_Business/Bills_Legislation/Bills_Search_Results/Result?bId=r6018

286 Ibid.

287 'Security of Critical Infrastructure (Consequential and Transitional Provisions) Bill 2018', viewed on 14 February 2019, https://www.aph.gov.au/Parliamentary_Business/Bills_Legislation/Bills_Search_Results/Result?bId=s1119

288 Peter Hatcher, 'Australia has 'woken up' the world on China's influence: US official', viewed on 14 February 2019, https://www.smh.com.au/politics/federal/australia-has-woken-up-the-world-on-china-s-influence-us-official-20180226-p4z1un.html

289 Ben Doherty and Eleanor Ainge Roy, 'Hillary Clinton says China's foreign power grab "a new global battle"', viewed on 14 February 2019, https://www.theguardian.com/us-news/2018/may/08/hillary-clinton-says-chinas-foreign-power-grab-a-new-global-battle

290 Craig Offman, 'CSIS warned this cabinet minister could be a threat. Ontario disagreed', viewed on 14 February 2019, https://www.theglobeandmail.com/news/national/csis-warned-this-cabinet-minister-could-be-a-threat-ontario-disagreed/article24974396/

291 Robert Fife and Steve Chase, 'Trudeau attended cash-for-access fundraiser with Chinese billionaires', viewed on 14 February 2019, https://www.theglobeandmail.com/news/politics/trudeau-attended-cash-for-access-fundraiser-with-chinese-billionaires/article32971362/

292 Ibid.

293 Fred Lum, 'Two Conservative senators' business venture linked to China', viewed on 14 February 2019, https://www.theglobeandmail.com/news/

politics/two-conservative-senators-business-venture-linked-to-china/article37340503/

294 'China detains third Canadian citizen since Huawei chief financial officer's arrest', viewed on 14 February 2019, https://www.abc.net.au/news/2018-12-20/china-detains-third-canadian-citizen-since-huawei-cfo-arrest/10636816

295 Patrick Wintour, 'Russian bid to influence Brexit vote detailed in new US Senate report', viewed on 14 February 2019, https://www.theguardian.com/world/2018/jan/10/russian-influence-brexit-vote-detailed-us-senate-report

296 Michael Auslin, 'Brexit Britain is eager for a sweet deal with Beijing. But at what price?', viewed on 14 February 2019, https://www.spectator.co.uk/2018/08/making-china-great-again/

297 Esha Vaish and Dasha Afanasieva, 'Chinese investment in London property is booming despite Brexit', viewed on 14 February 2019, https://www.businessinsider.com/r-hong-kong-property-investors-go-trophy-hunting-in-london-despite-brexit-2017-8?IR=T

298 Larry Diamond and Orville Schell, 'Chinese Influence and American Interests: Promoting Constructive Vigilance', viewed on 28 February 2019, https://www.hoover.org/research/chinese-influence-american-interests-promoting-constructive-vigilance

299 Jack Stubbs, 'UK says Huawei "shortcomings" expose telecom networks to security risks', viewed on 14 February 2019, https://www.afr.com/news/world/europe/uk-says-huawei-shortcomings-expose-telecom-networks-to-security-risks-20180720-h12x8x

300 Adam Vaughan and Lily Kuo, 'China's long game to dominate nuclear power relies on the UK', viewed on 14 February 2019, https://www.theguardian.com/environment/2018/jul/26/chinas-long-game-to-dominate-nuclear-power-relies-on-the-uk

301 'Putin lashes out at "traitor" ex-spy Sergei Skripal, denies involvement in poisoning', viewed on 14 February 2019, https://www.abc.net.au/news/2018-10-04/putin-calls-poisoned-ex-spy-sergei-skripal-a-scumbag/10335106

302 'Sharp Power: Rising Authoritarian Influence: New Forum Report – 5 December 2017' viewed on 31 January 2019 https://www.ned.org/sharp-power-rising-authoritarian-influence-forum-report/

303 Ibid.

304 Ibid.

305 Ibid.

306 'China formally opens first overseas military base in Djibouti', viewed on 13 February 2019, https://www.reuters.com/article/us-china-djibouti/china-formally-opens-first-overseas-military-base-in-djibouti-idUSKBN1A-H3E3

307 'How Russia is growing its strategic influence in Africa', viewed on 13 February 2019, http://theconversation.com/how-russia-is-growing-its-strategic-influence-in-africa-110930

308 'China signs 99-year lease on Sri Lanka's Hambantota port', viewed on 13 February 2019, https://www.ft.com/content/e150ef0c-de37-11e7-a8a4-0a1e63a52f9c

309 Soth Koemsoeun and Yesenia Amaro, 'Russia to send observers to Cambodia's 2018 election, agrees to discuss debt', viewed on 13 February 2019, https://www.phnompenhpost.com/national/russia-send-observers-cambodias-2018-election-agrees-discuss-debt

310 Oriana Skylar Mastro, 'The Stealth Superpower How China Hid Its Global Ambitions', viewed on 13 February 2019, https://www.foreignaffairs.com/articles/china/china-plan-rule-asia

311 Yuval Harari, 'Why Technology Favors Tyranny', viewed on 8 February 2019, https://www.theatlantic.com/magazine/archive/2018/10/yuval-noah-harari-technology-tyranny/568330/

312 Bret Stephens, 'The Rudderless West', viewed on 13 February 2019, https://www.nytimes.com/2019/01/17/opinion/brexit-western-powers.html

313 Graham Allison, *Destined for War* (Scribe, London, 2017), back cover.

314 *The Economist*, (October 27th 2018), 3.

315 Oriana Skylar Mastro and Jeane Kirkpatrick, 'The Stealth Superpower: How China Hid Its Global Ambitions', *Foreign Affairs*; New York Vol. 98, Iss. 1, (Jan/Feb 2019): 31.

316 Graham Allison, Destined for War (Scribe, London, 2017), 230-231.

317 Franklin Delano Roosevelt, Letter to His Excellency Adolf Hitler, Chancellor of the German Reich, 14 April 1939, viewed online 13 February 2019 <http://www.fdrlibrary.marist.edu/daybyday/resource/april-1939-7/>

Republic Earth Organisation

* 9 7 8 0 6 4 6 8 1 1 1 4 7 *